DATE DUE

GAYLORD			PRINTED IN U.S.A.

Jews in America

Religion in American Life

JON BUTLER & HARRY S. STOUT
GENERAL EDITORS

Jews in America

Hasia R. Diner

OXFORD UNIVERSITY PRESS
New York • Oxford

For my young, younger, and youngest readers—
Shira, Eli, and Matan

Oxford   New York
Athens Auckland Bangkok Bogotá   Buenos Aires
Calcutta   Cape Town Chennai Dar es Salaam
Delhi Florence Hong Kong Istanbul   Karachi
Kuala Lumpur Madrid Melbourne Mexico City
Mumbai Nairobi Paris São Paulo Singapore
Taipei Tokyo Toronto Warsaw

and associated companies in
Berlin   Ibadan

Published by Oxford University Press, Inc.
198 Madison Avenue, New York, New York 10016
Website: www.oup-usa.org

Oxford is a registered trademark of Oxford University Press

Library of Congress Cataloging-in-Publication Data

Diner, Hasia R.
Jews in America / Hasia R. Diner.
p. cm. — (Religion in American life)
Includes bibliographical references and index.
ISBN 0-19-510678-4 (edition)
1. Jews—United States—History—Juvenile literature. 2. Judaism—United States—
History—Juvenile literature. 3. United States—Ethnic relations—Juvenile literature.
[1. Jews—United States.] I. Title. II. Series.
E184.J5D4929 1998   973'.04924—dc21 98-17645

9 8 7 6 5 4 3 2 1

Printed in the United States of America
on acid-free paper

Design and layout: Loraine Machlin
Picture research: Lisa Kirchner

On the cover: Hannukah in New York *(detail)*, by Malcah Zeldis. Courtesy
Malcah Zeldis/Art Resource, NY.

Frontispiece: *A Judaica merchant in Washington, D.C. exhibits his patriotism*
in the shop's window display.

Contents

Introduction

JON BUTLER & HARRY S. STOUT, GENERAL EDITORS

The history of Jewish life in America dramatically illustrates how a religious group can adapt to a new culture and retain immense spiritual vitality. In the colonial period, America brought together the two great traditions of Judaism—Ashkenazic (Eastern European) and Sephardic (Spanish and Portuguese) Judaism. In the 19th and early 20th centuries, two unique Jewish denominational traditions emerged out of the American experience—the liberal Reform movement and the middle-of-the-road Conservative movement. They joined the Orthodox tradition as a part of the growing complexity of American Judaism. Reaction to the Holocaust and the Six-Day War in Israel in 1967 signaled renewed commitments to a united Jewish identity, not only in America but throughout the world.

But *Jews in America* is more than the story of how America shaped Jewish identity—it also vividly indicates how Judaism has helped shape America's religious identity. The first Jews in the British colonies proved that they could sustain a complex religious tradition with very few followers. As their numbers grew, they confirmed the importance of institutions, including denominational organizations and seminaries, and the significance of women in upholding and advancing American religion. And through a willingness to change, Jews revealed how religion would prosper in 20th century America despite the lure of secularized suburban life.

In 1865 the American Jews celebrated the festival of Purim with a charity ball.

This book is part of a unique 17-volume series that explores the evolution, character, and dynamics of religion in American life from 1500 to the end of the 20th century. As late as the 1960s, historians paid relatively little attention to religion beyond studies of New England's Puritans. But since then, American religious history and its contemporary expression have been the subject of intense inquiry. These new studies have thoroughly transformed our knowledge of almost every American religious group and have fully revised our understanding of religion's role in American history.

It is impossible to capture the flavor and character of the American experience without understanding the connections between secular activities and religion. Spirituality stood at the center of Native American societies before European colonization and has continued to do so long after. Religion—and the freedom to express it—motivated milllions of immigrants to come to America from remarkably different cultures, and the exposure to new ideas and ways of living shaped their experience. It also fueled tension among different ethnic and racial groups in America and, regretfully, accounted for difficult episodes of bigotry in American society. Religion urged Americans to expand the nation—first within the continental United States, then through overseas conquests and missionary work—and has had a profound influence on American politics, from the era of the Puritans to the present. Finally, religion contributes to the extraordinary diversity that has, for four centuries, made the United States one of the world's most dynamic societies.

The Religion in American Life series explores the historical traditions that have made religious freedom and spiritual exploration central features of American society. It emphasizes the experience of religion in America—what men and women have understood by religion, how it has affected politics and society, and how Americans have used it to shape their daily lives.

Chapter 1

First Journeys: 1654–1820

n late August or early September of 1654, a total of 23 Jews stepped from a ship onto the soil of what would one day be New York City, the largest Jewish community in the world. But in 1654 it was the Dutch city of New Amsterdam, and the 23 new arrivals were the first Jews there. Many of them scattered to other places soon thereafter, and all but one of them have disappeared from history. We know, however, that they had been traveling for a long time.

The Jews who arrived in New Amsterdam came from the Dutch colony of Recife in northeastern Brazil. A few generations earlier, however, their families had lived in Spain and Portugal on Europe's Iberian peninsula. These Iberian Jews were known as Sephardim (*Sepharad* is Hebrew for "Spain"). Under Muslim rule, the large and prosperous community of Spanish Jews created a rich culture in which tight-knit, all-Jewish communities enjoyed good relations with their Spanish neighbors.

But this Golden Age of Spanish Jewry ended in the 14th century when Christian rulers drove the Muslims out of Spain and began to persecute Jews. These rulers and the Roman Catholic Church wanted Spain to be an all-Christian society. They forced large numbers of Jews to convert to Christianity, often on pain of death. The authorities made it difficult for them to remain Jewish and live full lives in Spain. Most Jews

The Torah scroll, containing the Five Books of
Moses, is the sacred sym-
bol of Judaism. Jews fleeing
the persecutions in Spain
took Torah scrolls and
other ritual objects with
them as they sought
refuge throughout Europe.

refused to convert to Christianity, and in 1492 Queen Isabella of Spain ordered all Jews to leave the country forever, ending a thousand years of Jewish life there.

Yet many Spanish Jews did become Christians in order to remain in Spain. Of the 80,000 Jews on the Iberian peninsula, about half converted to Christianity rather than leave their homes. These converts were called New Christians or, in Spanish, *conversos*, although Christians sometimes called them by the insulting term *marranos*, meaning "pigs." The New Christians participated in Christian worship, but secretly, in the privacy of their homes, they tried to remain Jews. They faced many challenges. For example, although they could no longer follow the complicated and strict Jewish dietary laws known as *kashrut*, they did not want to eat pork, which Jews regard as an unclean meat—yet pork is a staple of Spanish cuisine. The New Christians had to abandon some Jewish customs completely. Following biblical direction, Jews had always circumcised their sons at eight days of age, physically marking Jewish boys as different from non-Jews. The New Christians had to stop doing this. They also had to stop giving their children Hebrew names and educating them as Jews.

In the 15th century the Catholic Church launched a campaign against the New Christians, accusing secret Jews of spreading dangerous ideas among "real" Christians that questioned basic church doctrines. Priests preached against the New Christians, and mobs attacked people suspected of being secret Jews. In 1483 the Church set up a permanent court called the Inquisition to investigate and stamp out challenges to its authority. Anyone could bring a charge before the Inquisition. The accused were held in dungeons, tortured while awaiting trial, and then usually executed.

The Inquisition was also active in neighboring Portugal, to which many *conversos* had fled. The position of the *conversos* grew even more frightening after Spain and Portugal united under a single monarchy in 1580. Another 10 years later a large group of New Christians fled Portugal for the city of Amsterdam in the Netherlands.

Amsterdam was attractive to Jews, who could worship freely there. Jews did not enjoy all of the benefits of citizenship available to Christians, but in general the Netherlands was religiously tolerant—a relief to the Jews after the persecution and secrecy of the Iberian peninsula. Many of the *conversos* who settled in Amsterdam returned to Judaism. They took Hebrew names, learned their traditions, and created full Jewish communities with rabbis, synagogues, Jewish schools, and Jewish cemeteries. They could obtain kosher meat and observe Jewish dietary laws. Men had themselves circumcised, making up for the years when they had been forced to hide their Jewishness and pretend to be something that they were not.

Amsterdam had another great advantage: It was a bustling center of international commerce, and commerce was familiar territory to the Jews. For centuries Jews in many parts of the world had been merchants instead of earning their living as farmers, like most other people; hatred and prejudice against Jews had led to laws that prevented them from owning land. The same prejudice kept most Jews out of the guilds, the organizations that craftsmen formed to protect their trades, and therefore few Jews could become skilled artisans. Instead the Jews bought and sold goods, traveling from place to place, buying up agricultural produce, and selling it in the cities. They also engaged in international trade, buying goods in the countries where they were produced and selling them in the countries where they were wanted. With few natural resources, the Netherlands had established

Some of the Jews who left Spain made their new home in Amsterdam, a relatively tolerant society that welcomed them, in part because of their extensive connections and experiences in international trade. This 1723 drawing depicts Amsterdam Jews at worship during the High Holiday of Rosh Hashanah.

In the early 17th century, Jews traveled on ships like this to the Americas. There, they relied upon those same ships for trading, their main occupation.

itself as an important center of international trade. Its wealth came from trade and it wanted more, which may be one reason why the Netherlands welcomed the Jews so warmly.

So the Jews in Amsterdam had a good life in a commercially active and religiously tolerant society. In the 1630s and 1640s a number of Jews joined other Dutch merchants and their families on journeys to the American colonies. By 1645 almost 1,500 Jews were living in the Dutch colonies in Brazil. In the town of Recife they built a synagogue for their congregation, which was called Zur Israel, "the rock of Israel." They brought a rabbi from Amsterdam, Isaac Aboab da Fonseca. A *haham*, or learned person, named Moses Rafael de Aguilar supervised a school.

In 1653 the Jews of Recife might have thought that their journeys had come to an end. They prospered economically from the trade in sugar and slaves that had built the colony. They experienced religious freedom. But in 1654 the Portuguese captured Recife. Within a few months— remembering the horrors of the Inquisition—all the Jews left. Some went back to Amsterdam. Others set sail for some of the Dutch islands of the Caribbean Sea. One group headed for the Dutch colony of Guyana on the north coast of South America. And 23 of the exiles decided to go to the northernmost Dutch American colony, New Netherland.

Two men met them on the docks of New Amsterdam, the colony's capital. One was Peter Stuyvesant, the director-general of the colony, and the other was Johannes Megapolensis, an official of the Dutch Reformed Church. Stuyvesant, a fervently religious man, and Megapolensis did not want anyone in the colony who did not belong to their church. They tried unsuccessfully to prevent the Jews from leaving the ship, just as they hoped to prevent members of other religions from settling in North America. In a letter to the colony's owner, the Dutch West India Company in Amsterdam, they accused Jews of being a "deceitful race" and practicing an "abominable religion." Stuyvesant asked the company what he should do with the Jews who had shown up on his doorstep.

The weary and penniless Jews also wrote to Amsterdam. They urged their fellow Jews, some of whom owned shares in the Dutch West India Company, to speak out on their behalf to the company and secure for them the right to remain in New Amsterdam.

On February 15, 1655, Stuyvesant and the Jews received their answer. It was a mixed message. The company's directors agreed with Stuyvesant's objections to the Jews and hoped that "the new territories should no more be allowed to be infected by people of the Jewish nation." But they also told Stuyvesant not to prevent the Jews from settling and trading in the colony. In a letter to Stuyvesant, the Dutch West India Company allowed the Jews to "quietly and peacefully carry on their business as before said and exercise in all quietness their religion within their houses." The Jews could enjoy the same privileges they had had in Amsterdam, although the company sternly warned them that they would have to take care of their own poor. Neither the company nor the colony of New Netherland would help them.

In 1655 and 1666 Stuyvesant issued many rulings that made life difficult for the Jews. They could not pray in public. They could not trade in the northern and southern reaches of the colony, nor could they become mechanics (skilled craftsmen or artisans) or sell real estate. Jews could not serve in the militia but had to pay a special tax to make up for not serving.

Despite Stuyvesant's and the Dutch West India Company's hostility toward Jews and their religion, the 23 Jewish immigrants—soon joined by other Sephardim from Amsterdam—set about creating a community in New Amsterdam. In 1655 the 13 adult Jewish males who lived there asked for, and received, the right to establish a cemetery. This was more important than having a synagogue. Jews can pray anywhere, and the Jewish residents of New Amsterdam probably prayed together in their homes. But a cemetery *had* to be maintained by the community. It meant that the Jews viewed this settlement as a permanent home—at least, as permanent as anything ever was in the history of the Jewish people.

Not all the Jews who settled in what would become the United States were Sephardim from Iberia. Some came to America after different journeys. German and Polish Jews, known as Ashkenazim, also settled in the American colonies. By the 1720s Ashkenazim outnumbered Sephardim in New York City (New Amsterdam had become New York in 1664 when the British captured the colony from the Dutch). By 1776, when the United States went to war seeking independence from Great Britain, Jews from Germany and Poland made up the majority of the American Jewish population.

Their experiences differed from those of the Sephardim. They could not look back to a "Golden Age" in their former homes. On the other hand, their families had not suffered persecution by the Inquisition or been forced to become secret Jews. Yet in Poland and northern Germany the Ashkenazim had known greater poverty than the Sephardim, and the Sephardim considered them to be of lower social status.

There were many differences between the two groups. The Ashkenazim spoke Yiddish, a Jewish language based on German and written in Hebrew characters, while the Sephardim spoke Spanish or Portuguese. When speaking Hebrew, the ancient language of the Jews, the two groups pronounced some words differently. Some other differences in the rituals, prayers, and customs of their religious services also set them apart from each other. For example, Sephardim held many ritual events such as circumcisions in the synagogue, but Ashkenazim celebrated these events in their homes. Finally, the Sephardim seemed to be less strict in their observance of Jewish law, perhaps because so many of them had once had to live as Christians or had enjoyed friendly relations with non-Jews.

The two groups were, however, more alike than they were different. Ashkenazim and Sephardim read from the same texts. One was the Torah, the first five books of the Hebrew Bible, which Jews consider to be the direct word of God. The other was the Talmud or Oral Law, a collection of rabbis' decisions on Jewish law, which tells Jews how to live. Ashkenazim and Sephardim followed the same Hebrew calendar. Both prayed in Hebrew. With minor variations their religious services were similar. Both groups observed the same laws of the Sabbath and *kashrut*. Both followed all the other details by which Jews organize their personal lives and those of their communities, circumcising their sons at eight days of age and observing laws of ritual purity, which meant that married women bathed in a *mikvah* (ritual bath) after menstruation so that they could resume sexual relations with their husbands. Ashkenazim and Sephardim celebrated the same holidays in basically the same ways: sounding the *shofar* (ram's horn) on Rosh Hashanah, the New Year; fasting on Yom Kippur, the day of atonement; eating an unleavened flat bread called *matzo* during Passover; lighting candles for eight nights during Hanukkah; building small huts during the fall holiday of Sukkoth, and many more.

For Jews to practice Judaism, they need many ritual objects. This board and knife were used in the 18th century by Jews in Newport, Rhode Island, to prepare matzo, the unleavened bread consumed during the eight-day holiday of Passover.

Like the Sephardim, the Ashkenazim had been driven from former homelands. Many German Jews had been forced to leave their homes after the Thirty Years' War (1618–48). The Jews of Poland had also suffered tremendously during that war, one of the most murderous periods in all of Jewish history. Many of the desperately poor Polish and German Jewish refugees fled to Amsterdam and London. Like the Netherlands, England was more tolerant of Jews and Judaism than the rest of Europe was.

In London and Amsterdam the Sephardim and Ashkenazim lived apart. To some extent the separation was economic—the Ashkenazim were generally poorer than the Sephardim. The two groups maintained separate synagogues, schools, cemeteries, burial societies, and other charitable institutions. Members of both communities seem to have been

Philadelphia was home to one of the six Jewish communities that formed before the American Revolution. Here, as in the other cities where Jews settled, access to waterways for merchant shipping was essential.

unhappy about marriages between Sephardim and Ashkenazim. They could not prevent such marriages, however—after all, Ashkenazim and Sephardim were both Jews, a unity that meant much more than any differences of social snobbery.

The Ashkenazim and Sephardim brought their ideas about each other to the Americas. Because the Sephardim were community leaders, all of the early American congregations followed the Sephardic form of worship, even when the majority of members were Ashkenazim. But the two groups did not live separately as they had in Europe. There were too few Jews in America. They had to stick together. In each city where Jews settled they formed one congregation that maintained a cemetery, charitable society, school, and ritual bath. The congregation also gave all Jews kosher meat and *matzo* for Passover.

Although people from both communities got upset when young Ashkenazim and Sephardim fell in love and decided to marry, the two groups stayed together as they founded and maintained Jewish institutions in America. Twice, however, Ashkenazim challenged the unity of the community and the Sephardic leadership. In Charleston, South Carolina, Ashkenazim had a separate congregation for a brief time in the 1780s, but the two groups soon reunited. A more permanent split took place in

Philadelphia in 1801 when a German Jewish group bought land for its own cemetery apart from the existing Jewish cemetery. No longer did the local Sephardic congregation represent all the Jews of Philadelphia.

The Jewish population in North America grew very slowly. The first 23 Jews arrived in 1654. By 1700 the number of Jews had risen to 200, by 1776 to 2,500, and by 1820 to 4,000. Most of the Jews lived along the Atlantic coast, creating Jewish communities in such port cities as New York; Newport, Rhode Island; Savannah, Georgia; Charleston, South Carolina; and Philadelphia.

Each of these communities has its own history, but in many ways they were similar. Regardless of where they lived, nearly all Jews earned their living as merchants. Typically they owned small stores that sold hardware, candles, dry goods, and liquor. Larger, more successful merchants also shipped raw materials such as timber, grain, furs, molasses, and tobacco to Europe and imported manufactured goods such as cloth and ironware for sale to Americans. A few of the very wealthiest participated in the slave trade that brought African slaves to the Americas and West Indian rum and molasses to North America. Most Jews, however, owned and worked in small stores that were family businesses. Men and women, adults and children shared the effort of making a living.

Another way in which American Jewish communities resembled one another is that all of them looked to Europe for some of their basic needs. For example, if Jews needed a Torah scroll, prayer books, or other *klay kodesh* (holy objects), they had to import these items from abroad. They also had to import a special kind of knowledge—the decisions of rabbis. In Jewish tradition, a rabbi was a scholar, teacher, judge, and authority on *halakah* (Jewish law). Rabbis decided questions about religious practice, and individual Jews as well as whole communities turned to rabbis when they did not know what the law required of them. But no rabbis had chosen to lived in America until 1840, well after the end of the colonial period. When questions of Jewish law arose, early American Jewish congregations wrote to rabbis in Amsterdam or London requesting rulings.

Because rabbis seldom led religious services or gave sermons, American Jews could carry on routine religious practice without them. Any male Jew could lead a service. Most early congregations did employ a *chazzan* or cantor, who chanted the service. When they could, congregations also hired a *shochet,* who slaughtered livestock according to Jewish law, and a *mohel,* who performed circumcisions.

But the real power in the Jewish communities of early America lay in the hands of the *parnassim,* wealthy merchants who served as trustees of the congregation. A board of trustees elected a *parnass,* who made basic decisions about the congregation's affairs and the lives of its members. The *parnass* strictly enforced Jewish law and made sure that only members in good standing received the benefits of the congregation. Because the single synagogue in the city administered all community services to the Jewish population, the *parnass* had a great deal of power. He could deny individual Jews the right to marriage, circumcision of sons, burial, kosher meat, *matzo,* and charitable assistance during times of need. In the 1770s, for example, the *parnass* of New York's Shearith Israel had a long argument with Hetty Hays, the owner of a boardinghouse. The *parnass* claimed that Hays had been serving non-kosher meat, but she refused to allow a visiting rabbi from London to inspect her kitchen.

In America, Jews moved around a lot. A Jewish couple in New York might have children living in Newport, Philadelphia, and Charleston, in parts of the West Indies such as Antigua, Barbados, and Jamaica, or in London. Jews also helped each other in trade. Some migrated to places that already had small Jewish communities because a relative or friend had encouraged them to pursue economic opportunities there. Others went to developing frontier settlements such as Albany, New York; Cumberland, Maryland; or Cincinnati, Ohio—places that had no Jews.

Solitary, far-ranging Jewish merchants and traders made their way to some of the most remote areas of North America, often long before permanent white settlements were established. As early as 1658 Asser Levy— one of the original 23 Jews who had come to New Amsterdam—owned property in the frontier outpost of Albany and had acquired the rights of a burgher, or citizen. Other Jews showed up there in 1678 and 1761, but not until the early 1830s did enough Jews live in Albany to make up a community. Similarly, a few lone Jews reached the headwaters of the James River in Virginia in the 1650s, but the first Jewish settlers did not arrive there until 1769. A congregation in Richmond is mentioned in a 1790 letter congratulating Virginian George Washington on his inauguration as the first President of the United States.

Nearly all of the congregations that served the early American Jews began as informal groups. It took time for the Jews to decide that they were staying in America and needed permanent institutions. This decision often took place when the Jews of a community realized that they needed a cemetery. Then they organized themselves into a congregation. But Jewish tradition did not require people to worship in a building specifically designated as a synagogue, and sometimes years passed before a community of Jews decided that they needed a synagogue.

The story of a Philadelphia congregation shows how Jewish institutions came into being. By the 1730s a group of Jews, mostly Ashkenazim, lived and traded in Philadelphia but had not taken any steps to create an organized Jewish community. In 1738 the son of a man named Nathan Levy died. Levy had no place to bury the boy according to Jewish tradition, so he bought a piece of land. At first, it seems, this plot was a family burial ground, but by the early 1740s it belonged to a loosely linked Jewish community that met for prayer on the Sabbath and holidays. The next step took place in 1761, when a group of Philadelphia Jews received a Torah scroll on permanent loan from a New York congregation. The Philadelphia Jews began to hold religious services in a private home in Sterling Alley. In 1771 they rented a space on Cherry Alley and gave their congregation a name: Kahal Kodesh Mikve Israel, "the holy congregation the hope of Israel." Two years later they applied to colonial officials for a formal charter.

By and large the few Jews in Philadelphia, New York, Newport, Charleston, and Savannah got along quite well with their non-Jewish neighbors. Still, the hatred that many European Christians felt toward

Jews had not disappeared as Europeans became Americans. Ministers—particularly in Massachusetts—delivered sermons against the Jews, blaming them for the crucifixion of Jesus and calling them agents of Satan. In a 1669 book entitled *The Mystery of Israel's Salvation,* Boston minister Increase Mather declared that the Jews carried the sin of killing Jesus and that they bore "the guilt of the blood of the Savior." Colonial newspapers at times presented stereotypes of Jews as dirty and greedy. During the American Revolution, for example, the *Charleston Gazette* claimed that the Jews were collaborating with the British to make money.

Just as in Europe, Jews in America faced limits on their rights and freedoms. In the 18th century Jews could not live in Massachusetts, Connecticut, or New Hampshire. In most of the colonies and later some of the states, Jews could not vote, hold elected office, or serve on juries. These restrictions did not single out Jews. They applied to anyone who did not belong to the established, or official, Christian church—the Anglican church in some places, the Congregational in others. Catholics, Quakers, and members of other religious minorities suffered as much as Jews from laws that tied political rights to religious affiliation.

Despite some prejudice and religious intolerance, American Jews in the 17th and 18th centuries had more freedom and fewer problems than any other Jews in the world. The special circumstances of life in colonial America and the early United States favored the acceptance of Jews and their religious traditions. Before and after the Revolution, America was a raw, growing place that welcomed people who were willing to contribute to the economy. Trade kept the colonies alive and made them prosperous. The Jews brought useful commercial skills and experiences that colonial administrators and ordinary people valued. Furthermore, the Jews were not the only religious and ethnic "outsiders" in early America. Like the Jews, the Catholics, Quakers, Methodists, Anabaptists, Mennonites, and other smaller groups quietly challenged the idea that only members of the established church could be accepted members of society. German, Irish, French, Welsh, and Scottish settlers—as well as Jews—created an ethnically diverse society in which different kinds of people could both participate in public life and band together in their own communities.

One other aspect of life in America was sigificant to the Jews. In all the other places where Jews had lived, the non-Jewish majority had regarded them as the lowest group in society. But as free people with white skin, Jews in America enjoyed privileges denied to blacks. For the first time, the Jews were not the most "different" part of the population.

In fact, Jews did not stand out as terribly different from other early Americans. They made deliberate efforts to blend in, not wanting to call attention to themselves or appear out of step with the society around them. Within their own communities they worshipped as they always had, ate kosher food, and educated their children in their traditions. But on the outside they looked just like the people around them. They did not dress differently. In fact, as time went on Jews in America abandoned some traditional practices when they followed the customs of the larger society: Men began shaving their beards and uncovering their heads, women started wearing modern dresses with low necklines, and married women appeared in public without hair coverings.

When the Jews finally began to build synagogues they again chose to blend in, not stand out. The oldest synagogue building in the United States, Jehuat Israel in Newport, Rhode Island, looks just like many churches and public buildings of its time. Dedicated in 1763, Jeshuat Israel is popularly known as the Touro Synagogue in honor of Isaac Touro, its first leader, and his son, Judah, who provided funds to support the congregation. The synagogue was built in the Palladian style, a popular 18th-century architectural style based on Roman buildings. Its columns and pediments emphasized balance, symmetry, and elegance. From the street an observer would have never known what took place inside. No markings or signs identified the building as Jewish.

Life in early America was good to the Jews—probably better than any life they had known since the Romans drove them out of their national homeland in c.e. 70. America was more tolerant than any place the Jews had known, with the possible exception of Spain in the "Golden Age." In America Jews interacted freely with others around them. Jews and Gentiles (non-Jews) established business partnerships and socialized in their leisure hours. For example, Joseph Simon, a Jewish frontier trader in

George Washington Writes the Hebrew Congregation in New Port, Rhode Island, 1790

While Jews were notable in the American colonies as non-Christians, the level of restriction against them never equaled that of Europe. In the age of the American Revolution, Jews felt a great deal of comfort that the leaders of the United States did not exclude them. During George Washington's visited to New Port (now Newport) in 1790 ,he met with members of town's Hebrew congregation, and the ensuing exchange of letters testifies to the civil equality granted to all Americans.

While I receive with much satisfaction your address replete with expressions of affection and esteem, I rejoice in the opportunity of assuring you that I shall always retain a grateful remembrance of the cordial welcome I experienced in my visit to New Port from all classes of Citizens.

The reflection on the days of difficulty and danger which are past is rendered the more sweet from a consciousness that they are succeeded by days of uncommon prosperity and security.

If we have wisdom to make the best use of the advantages with which we are now favored, we cannot fail, under the just administration of a good government, to become a great and happy people.

The Citizens of the United States of America have a right to applaud themselves for having given to mankind examples of an enlarged and liberal policy, a policy worthy of imitation. All possess alike liberty of conscience and immunities of citizenship.

It is now no more that toleration is spoken of as if it was by the indulgence of one class of people, that another enjoyed the exercise of their inherent natural rights. For happily the government of the United States, which gives to bigotry no sanction, to persecution no assistance, requires only that they who live under its protection should demean themselves as good citizens, in giving it on all occasions their effectual support.

It would be inconsistent with the frankness of my character not to avow that I am pleased with your favorable opinion of my administration, and fervent wishes for my felicity.

Peter Harrison, who had designed several churches in North America, designed the Touro Synagogue (dedicated in 1763) for Jews in Newport, Rhode Island. On the inside it replicated the style of the Spanish-Portuguese synagogue in Amsterdam.

May the children of the Stock of Abraham, who dwell in this land, continue to merit and enjoy the good will of the other inhabitants, while every one shall sit in safety under his own vine and fig-tree and there shall be none to make him afraid.

COMMEMORATING
FRANCIS SALVADOR
1747-1776

FIRST JEW IN SOUTH CAROLINA TO HOLD PUBLIC OFFICE
AND
TO DIE FOR AMERICAN INDEPENDENCE

HE CAME TO CHARLES TOWN FROM HIS NATIVE
LONDON IN 1773 TO DEVELOP EXTENSIVE FAMILY
LANDHOLDINGS IN THE FRONTIER DISTRICT OF
NINETY SIX. AS A DEPUTY TO THE PROVINCIAL
CONGRESSES OF SOUTH CAROLINA, 1775 AND 1776,
HE SERVED WITH DISTINCTION IN THE CREATION
OF THIS STATE AND NATION. PARTICIPATING AS
A VOLUNTEER IN AN EXPEDITION AGAINST INDIANS
AND TORIES, HE WAS KILLED FROM AMBUSH NEAR
THE KEOWEE RIVER, AUGUST 1, 1776.

BORN AN ARISTOCRAT, HE BECAME A DEMOCRAT;
AN ENGLISHMAN, HE CAST HIS LOT WITH AMERICA;
TRUE TO HIS ANCIENT FAITH, HE GAVE HIS LIFE
FOR NEW HOPES OF HUMAN LIBERTY AND UNDERSTANDING.

ERECTED AT THE TIME OF THE BICENTENNIAL CELEBRATION
OF THE JEWISH COMMUNITY OF CHARLESTON, 1950.

APPROVED BY THE HISTORICAL COMMISSION OF CHARLESTON, S.C.

This marker outside the city hall of Charleston, South Carolina, honors the memory of Francis Salvador, a Jew who served in the South Carolina Provincial Congress in the years immediately surrounding the American Revolution. He fell in battle on August 1, 1776.

western Pennsylvania, shared a 40-year partnership with Colonel Alexander Lowry, a non-Jew, trading with Indians. Simon also had business partnerships with several other Gentiles as well as with Jews.

So freely did Jews mingle with their Christian neighbors that many marriages between Jews and Christians took place. Sometimes the Gentile spouse in these marriages converted to Judaism, and sometimes the Jewish spouse remained in the Jewish community. Most often, however, Jews who married Christians joined the Christian majority.

The story of Abigail Franks shows how comfortable Jews could be in 18th-century America—and the problems that went along with this comfort. Abigail was the daughter of a New York merchant named Moses Levy. Sometime around 1712 she married Jacob Franks, who had recently come to America from England. Like Abigail's father, her husband succeeded in his many business ventures. Their sons went into business, too. Abigail wrote many letters to them as they went off on their commercial ventures, always reminding them to remain true to their Jewish traditions. Her letters also described her social life, which included visits to non-Jewish friends. Abigail spent some summers vacationing with these friends. But when her daughter married Oliver Delancey, a Christian, she kept the marriage a secret for six months because she was so ashamed. Abigail Franks never agreed to meet her son-in-law. In her view, marrying a Gentile was going too far.

The Jewish experience in America had started off on shaky grounds. Peter Stuyvesant gave the first group of Jews a less than friendly welcome on the wharf of New Amsterdam's harbor. But during the 17th and 18th centuries American Jews came to identify with their homes and neighbors, and when Americans challenged Great Britain and declared their independence, most Jews enthusiastically joined the patriot cause. Many men volunteered for the army. Jews in South Carolina, for example, formed a self-proclaimed "Jew Company." A Jewish doctor helped provide medical relief to the troops at Valley Forge, and Jewish merchants supplied goods to the Continental Army. Mordecai Sheftell of Savannah tried to bring goods to the American people by running the blockade that the British navy had set up to close American ports. The British captured him, jailed him on a prison ship, and then exiled him to the island of Antigua.

One Jew who played an important part in revolutionary affairs was Haym Salomon. Born in Poland, Salomon came to New York in the 1770s. By 1781 he was in Philadelphia, a center of the patriot cause, serving as an assistant to Robert Morris, the superintendent of the Office of Finance of the United States. Salomon loaned money to the Continental Congress without interest, and James Madison praised Salomon for helping the struggling revolutionary cause.

The Revolution did not instantly change the status of Jews in America, but it started a process that dramatically altered their lives. Once they had won their independence from England and joined in the federation called the United States, the various former colonies had to rewrite the laws by which they governed themselves. Starting with New York in 1777, many states guaranteed religious freedom to all. By the 1820s the last traces of state-level discrimination against Jews had vanished, except in North Carolina.

Perhaps more important, the federal Constitution of 1789 made it possible for Jews to enjoy the full benefits of American life. Article 6, section 3 of the Constitution stated that "no religious test shall ever be required as a qualification to any office or public trust under the

David and Phila Franks were the children of Jacob and Abigail Levy Franks. Their father was one of the most influential and successful Jews of 18th-century New York.

In Savannah, Georgia, Jewish merchant Mordecai Sheftell (above) and his partner Philip Minis played an active role in the revolutionary war efforts. The British authorities denounced Sheftell and Minis for their participation in that resistance and cited their Jewishness as noteworthy.

United States." This meant that when it came to serving in Congress, the army, the diplomatic service, or even the Presidency, religion could never disqualify anyone for federal office. (The Fourteenth Amendment, passed in 1865 after the Civil War, required that state laws not "abridge the privileges" of any citizens of the United States.)

Perhaps the most important part of the Constitution for Jews was the First Amendment, the first section of what we have come to know as the Bill of Rights, which said: "Congress shall make no law respecting an establishment of religion, or prohibiting the free exercise thereof." Ever since these words were written, courts have debated how to interpret "establishment" and "free exercise" in practical situations. But the Constitution's commitment to religious neutrality opened up a new era for Jews.

In 1788 the *chazzan* of Philadelphia's Mikve Israel congregation was invited to join the Fourth of July parade that celebrated Pennsylvania's ratification of the Constitution of the United States. He marched down the city's main street arm-in-arm with two Protestant clergymen. Organizers of the parade had prepared a special table, abounding in kosher food, for the city's Jews. All faiths were equal in the new nation—at least in the eyes of the law.

The changes brought by the Revolution and the Constitution did not affect only the Jews' relations with Gentiles. They also shook up Jewish communities. Taking their cues from the society around them, in which political life had opened up to allow broader participation, Jews began to make their congregations more democratic. Many congregations wrote constitutions for themselves, using words and phrases associated with the Revolutionary period. The new constitution of New York's Shearith Israel congregation, for example, began, "Whereas in free states all power originates and is derived from the people. . . ." Many synagogues took exclusive power away from the *parnassim* and allowed all adult men to vote on synagogue matters. Instead of fining people who had violated Jewish law, congregations appealed to members' goodwill and conscience to ensure observance of the law.

American Jews stopped thinking of synagogues as places where they had to belong, with rules they had to follow. The synagogue became a voluntary institution that individual Jews joined because they chose to. The more Jews came to regard synagogue membership as voluntary, the more synagogues had to respect the wishes of members. Soon those members would depart from tradition.

After the Revolution new Jewish communities formed in recently opened-up parts of the young country. From the 1770s through 1820 Jewish congregations formed in Richmond, Virginia; New Orleans, Louisiana; Cincinnati, Ohio; Baltimore, Maryland; and a string of other places. Jews no longer limited themselves to coastal communities. As they started their journeys, they no longer looked to Europe for guidance in how to be Jewish. The Jews of America felt free to create the institutions they wanted.

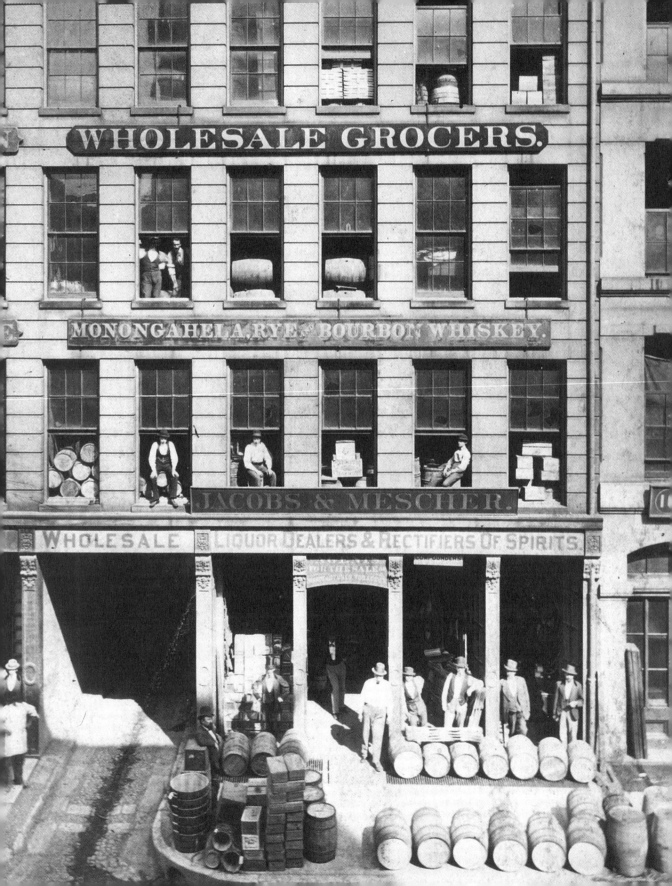

Chapter 2

Across America: 1820–1880

On June 15, 1842, Abraham Kohn left his home village in Bavaria, southern Germany. He confessed to his diary, "I wept bitterly as I kissed my dear mother, perhaps for the last time, in Wittelshofen, pressing her hand and commending her to the protection of the Eternal, the Father of all widows and orphans." Kohn was not alone. A childhood friend and his brother Moses accompanied him. They were just three of the thousands of young Jewish women and men who left their European homes in the mid-19th century. Small groups of siblings and friends, mostly young unmarried people, abandoned the villages of southern and western Germany, Alsace, Bohemia, Hungary, Posen, Lithuania, and western Russia to seek opportunities in America.

The mass migration of young Jews from central Europe—the area between France and Russia—began in the 1820s. By 1880 about 150,000 Jews from central Europe had come to the United States. Life in this part of Europe was deteriorating for the Jews, most of whom were poor villagers and not particularly well educated. In the past, they had eked out a living through peddling, other kinds of small-time commerce, and crafts, but these occupations could support them no longer. Europe was industrializing. Railroads and other improvements in communication and transportation meant that traveling peddlers were not needed to move goods from place to place. At the same time, the old hostility of

Cincinnati was the first Jewish community to be founded west of the Appalachian Mountains. Jewish immigrants settled there because of commercial opportunities. They made a living in wholesale and retail business and ran shops selling groceries, liquor, clothes, and dry goods.

Christians toward Jews was increasing. And many young Jewish men left their home countries to avoid being drafted into the army.

The ocean crossing to the United States took about six weeks, depending upon the weather. Most ships docked in New York, but some went to Baltimore, New Orleans, or Philadelphia. Many of the new arrivals already knew someone living in the United States. They spent their first days in the new country reuniting with friends and family.

Abraham Kohn arrived in New York from Bavaria the day before the beginning of Rosh Hashanah, the Jewish New Year. The timing seemed promising: Kohn wrote of a new year, a "new career before me," in a new home. He prayed at the new Attorney Street Synagogue, Congregation Shaar Hashomayim ("the gates of heaven") on New York's Lower East Side. On this self-reflective holiday, which calls Jews to take stock of their deeds during the past year and prepare for the new one, Kohn's thoughts turned to both his past and his future. He wrote in his diary, "I prayed to the almighty, thanking him for the voyage happily finished and asking good and abiding health for my dear mother and brothers and sisters. I prayed then for my own good health and asked for all of us good fortune. May the dear Lord hear my prayer! May he bless and bestow upon us his infinite mercy and charity! Amen."

Like most immigrants, Kohn faced the problem of making a living. Unable to get a job as a store clerk, he did what countless other young Jewish men had done. He became a peddler. These men put packs—sometimes weighing as much as 100 pounds—on their backs and began new American journeys, carrying pots and pans, needles and thread, mirrors, fabric, and sometimes even stoves and furniture. Some walked. Those with a little money rode on horse-drawn wagons. They staked out routes in the South, Pennsylvania, West Virginia, or the Midwest, and some of them made it all the way to California and Nevada. Abraham Kohn chose to peddle in New England, with Boston as the base where he stocked up on supplies. Later he went west to Chicago.

Wherever they peddled, whatever goods they sold, Jews filled a special place in the American economy. Americans lived spread out across the countryside, on small farms relatively far from towns and cities. Many could not easily go to stores. But if American farmers could not get to the goods they needed, the goods came to them, strapped to the back of a young Jewish immigrant.

At first these young men spoke no English at all. During the week they walked the roads from farmhouse to farmhouse. Doors sometimes slammed in their faces. Local children threw stones at them. Robbers attacked them. A few robberies became murders, and the young Jewish immigrant ended up dead on a lonely stretch of road in some isolated region, far from family or from a community that could perform its last act toward him: proper Jewish burial.

No matter if the weather turned cold or temperatures soared—the peddlers had to be out there selling their goods. Usually they slept outdoors. A friendly farmer might offer them a barn for the night, and a very generous one might offer a real bed in the house, in front of a warm fire. Abraham Kohn recorded in his diary how, on the night of a heavy snowfall, a housewife had told her husband not to let the peddler stay the night. "She was afraid of strangers . . . we should go our way," Kohn wrote. "And outside there raged the worst blizzard I have ever seen. O God, I thought, is this the land of liberty and hospitality and tolerance?" Eventually, the woman changed her mind and let the peddler stay.

On Friday afternoons the Jewish peddlers tried to congregate in towns or cities that had Jewish communities. There they might find a synagogue, a kosher boardinghouse, or a congenial group of fellow Jews with whom they could pray and eat and relax. They could mark the Sabbath in the company of other Jews, and they could rest—the meaning of Sabbath—before they resumed their arduous routes. Usually, however, circumstances prevented them from observing the seventh day and keeping it holy, and few boardinghouses offered kosher food.

Peddling represented the lowest rung in Jewish commerce. Thousands of young Jewish men in America went door-to-door selling goods to families. This peddler in Ohio was lucky. He had a horse and wagon and did not have to carry his goods on his back.

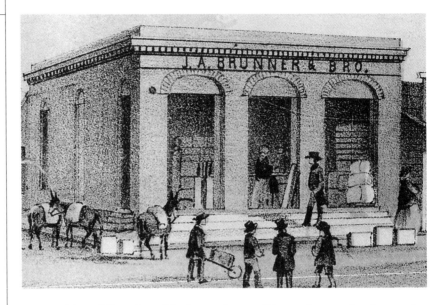

Jews from Central Europe made their way all across the American continent, going wherever they thought they might be able to make a living. In the mid-1850s, the Brunner brothers opened their store in Jacksonville, Oregon, near the gold fields.

Jewish peddlers found it almost impossible to observe the day-to-day details of proper Jewish life. Rules about food vexed the peddlers most. According to *kashrut,* Jews could eat the flesh of some animals but not others. Pork, the most common meat in the American diet, was forbidden. Meat had to be slaughtered in a very specific way by a *shochet.* Jews could not eat meat and milk at the same meal. Many found it easier to give up *kashrut,* and those who would not do so often lived as vegetarians. Peddlers reported that some of the Cherokee Indians of North Carolina called the Jews they met "egg eaters."

Peddling was a hard, lonely, and often dangerous job. But for many Jews it was the first step to a more settled future. Peddling was the basis for the creation of dozens of Jewish communities across the United States. After the peddlers had been in the United States for a few years and had developed trading routes, they sent money to Europe so that brothers, cousins, nephews, or friends could join them. With their help the peddler could expand his business, penetrating deeper and deeper into the American hinterlands.

Moderately successful Jewish peddlers saved some money and opened small stores in little towns and medium-sized cities. Such towns typically had a few Jewish-owned stores, almost all selling the same kind of items, clustered in the downtown districts. Merchants usually lived above or behind their stores.

The moment when a peddler traded in his pack for a merchant's apron was a turning point in the formation of Jewish communities all over the United States. When a peddler had enough capital to open a store he usually got married, sometimes going back to his former home village in Europe to find a bride—and also to show off a bit and let the townspeople who had known him as a lad see how well he had done in his new home. He would then take his bride—and quite often a few other unmarried young Jewish women—back to the United States. The other women almost always married other former peddlers who were now opening up their stores. These newly married shopkeepers did not completely give up their peddling careers. Many of them continued to sell directly to the farmers while their wives and children tended the stores.

Jewish women from central Europe had grown up in a tradition in which wives and daughters worked. In both Europe and the United States Jews made a living—just barely—in small businesses that required everybody's labor. In most cases women worked in the family store, "helping out." But sometimes women made the important decisions, and many of them had their own businesses, independent of their husbands.

Some Jewish women, often widows, ran boardinghouses for the peddlers and other single immigrant men who needed a place to stay. Other women operated their own stores in their own names. Sarah Goldwater, who lived in California's Tuolumne County in the 1860s, did not want to be responsible for her husband's debts, so she filed a statement with the courthouse, saying, "from and after this date I intend to carry on and transact in my own name and on my own account, the business of tailoring and merchandising. . . . I will be personally responsible for all debts contracted by me in said business."

Throughout the 1830s and 1840s former peddlers and their shopkeeping wives settled down in places like Albany, Rochester, Syracuse, Buffalo, and Utica, New York; Memphis, Tennessee; St. Louis, Missouri; Sioux City, Iowa; Milwaukee, Wisconsin; Cleveland, Columbus, Akron, and Cincinnati, Ohio; Minneapolis, Minnesota; Louisville and Lexington,

The pleasure of your company is respectfully solicited to be present at the Wedding Party of

Simon Baum and Miss Marjana Bettman,

to take place at the residence of

MR. H. L. BLAUM, JR.

Sunday Sept 19, at 1 o'clk P. M.

1858

Simon Baum and Marjana Bettman, the first Jews to be married in Oregon, sent out invitations to their 1858 wedding. The arrival of Jewish women and the birth of children ensured the establishment of permanent communities.

Kentucky; Washington, D.C.; Portland, Maine; Portland, Oregon; and dozens of other cities. Jewish merchants opened some of the first shops in Los Angeles, San Francisco, Denver, and Detroit. Over time these cities developed full Jewish communities with synagogues, schools, cemeteries, charitable societies, and places of recreation.

After some Jews had settled in a town, that town drew other Jews—first from the same part of Europe as the original settlers, but within a decade or two from other regions. Jews came to these communities because they knew they would not be alone. In Chicago, for example, documents from the 1830s—city directories, newspaper subscription lists, advertisements, and voters' lists—show four or five Jews living in the raw frontier town that was still troubled by roaming bears. Twenty Jewish immigrants arrived between 1840 and 1844. In 1845 they established a cemetery, and the men formed a *minyan*, the group of at least 10 people needed for prayer services. That year's Yom Kippur service took place above a store. Soon afterward 14 Jewish men formally incorporated into a congregation, the first in the Midwest. They called themselves Kehilath Anshe Ma'ariv (KAM), "the congregation of the men of the west." The founders of KAM wrote to other Jewish congregations in the United States for help getting started, something that most new, struggling congregations did. In 1847 Chicago's Jews hired a *shochet* and a *ba'al koreh,* a Torah reader. In 1851 they dedicated their first synagogue building and opened a day school to teach their children.

Most of the first Jews who settled Chicago, soon to be called "America's Second City," came from Bavaria. Beginning in the 1840s they were joined by Jews from Bohemia, Poland, and Lithuania. Each group formed its own congregation, consecrated its own cemetery ground, and lived in a somewhat separate neighborhood, at least at first. Jewish life in American towns and cities reflected European regional differences, but in most communities Jews banded together to form associations to take care of those in need. Regardless of where Jews came from, they believed it was everyone's responsibility to provide orphanages, job-information services, free coal, food for the hungry, *matzo* at Passover, dowries to help poor girls get married, hospitality to travelers, and support for impoverished widows. They created and supported institutions to provide these services.

Soon, however, American Jews began to be divided by differences that had nothing to do with their nation of origin. Some Jews had strayed from strict observance of Jewish tradition, perhaps because they had spent so many years as peddlers and could not follow the many laws of Judaism. Most American Jews became rather flexible about Jewish

Throughout America Jewish women gathered together to form mutual aid and charitable societies. This group in Arizona, like most of the others, called itself the Hebrew Ladies' Benevolent Society.

practice. They did not mind the idea of modifying some parts of tradition under new conditions.

And there were Jews who were eager to change aspects of Judaism. Starting in the early 19th century, some Jews in Germany and the United States believed that Judaism had to be completely changed, or reformed. They intended to bring Judaism into line with 19th-century rationalism, a way of thought that emphasized science, reason, and progress, and they wanted to do away with parts of the faith that did not seem to fit modern knowledge. For example, in their traditional prayers, Jews pray for a day when the dead will come back to life. Reformers eliminated this prayer because logic and science say that the dead cannot be resurrected. Supporters of reform also wanted Jewish religious ritual to have more decorum—to be more orderly and more artistically beautiful.

In Chicago in 1861 a group of Reform Jews followed Dr. Bernhard Felsenthal out of Kehilath Anshe Ma'ariv to found the Reform Sinai Temple. They made profound changes in the ways Jews prayed and lived, stressing the need to update Jewish practice and to get rid of things that seemed not to make sense or that differed too sharply from the customs

David Kokernot served in the Army of the Confederacy during the Civil War. Jewish men fought for either the Union or the Confederacy depending upon where they lived.

of Christians. The Chicago reformers wanted Jews to hold their main religious service on Sunday rather than Saturday, and they found the traditional Jewish practice of having men and women sit in separate sections of the synagogue to be out of step with the world around them. They liked the idea of adding an organ to religious worship, and they wanted to drop prayers whose words and sentiments they did not agree with.

Not all Jews supported these changes. Some resisted changes and even left congregations that they thought were changing too much. When the Washington Hebrew Congregation in the nation's capital added an organ in 1877, a traditional group left to found Adas Israel. The traditionalists called themselves Orthodox.

Orthodox devotion to tradition is represented by Abraham Rice, who came to the United States from

Bavaria in 1840. The first ordained rabbi in this country, Rice came to serve a congregation in Baltimore. Almost from the beginning Rice disliked the United States. He believed—perhaps rightly—that conditions there made it very difficult for Jews to practice traditional Judaism. Rice wrote to a friend and teacher in Germany, "I live in complete darkness. . . . The religious life in this land is on the lowest level, most people eat foul food and desecrate the Sabbath in public. . . . Thousands marry non-Jewish women. . . . I wonder whether it is even permissible for a Jew to live in this land."

Another rabbi played a key role in developing American Reform Judaism. He was Isaac Mayer Wise, the rabbi of Cincinnati's Kehilat Kadosh Bene Yeshurun, "the holy congregation of the children of Jeshurun," and he took a middle position between radical Reformers and

Sculptor Moses Ezekiel works on a bust of Isaac Meyer Wise in 1899. By this time, Wise reigned as the undisputed leader of American Reform Judaism and had already founded the three crucial institutions of the movement: the Union of American Hebrew Congregations, the Hebrew Union College, and the Central Conference of American Rabbis.

מורה דרך

ללמד את נערי בני ישראל דרכי לשון עברית

THE

HEBREW READER:

HEBREW AND ENGLISH.

DESIGNED

AS AN EASY GUIDE TO THE HEBREW TONGUE,

FOR

JEWISH CHILDREN AND SELF-INSTRUCTION.

NO. I.
THE SPELLING BOOK.

BY ISAAC LEESER.

PHILADELPHIA:
PRINTED BY HASWELL, BARRINGTON, AND HASWELL.
1838.

In 1838, Isaac Leeser of Philadelphia's Mikveh Israel published the first American textbook to teach the Hebrew language. This book, like many of his other publications, was aimed at Jewish children.

the strict Orthodox. Wise, who came from Bohemia in 1846, claimed to have been ordained as a rabbi in Germany, but his critics always noted that he could not prove it.

Wise believed strongly that Judaism had to modernize and come up to date. If Judaism in the United States did not fit in with American culture, young American Jews would be less loyal to their faith and less willing to participate in Jewish religion and Jewish communities. For example, if Jews continued to pray for a return to their ancient homeland, then American Jews who were happy in the United States would separate from Judaism. Wise also was convinced, after visiting Jewish communities in large cities and small towns, that American Jews needed to have rabbis who were trained in the United States, fluent in English, in step with American values, and scientific in their approach. He wanted all American Jews, wherever they came from, to use the same prayer book and pray according to the same religious ritual. In 1856 he published this ritual, which he called *Minhag America* (The American Rite).

Some Reformers claimed that Wise did not go far enough. Led by Rabbi David Einhorn of Baltimore and then New York, the extreme Reformers criticized Wise. The Orthodox, led by Isaac Leeser, the *chazzan* of Philadelphia's Mikveh Israel, also criticized him—this time for being too willing to abandon key elements of Jewish practice.

Despite criticism from extremists on both sides, Wise created three enduring institutions that became the heart of American Reform Judaism. In 1873 he created the Union of American Hebrew Congregations, which included the congregations that followed his ideas. In 1875 he welcomed the first class to the Hebrew Union College (HUC), a training school for American rabbis in Cincinnati. In 1889 he led graduates of HUC and others in the formation of the Central Conference of American Rabbis, an association of rabbis who identified with the Reform movement.

But most of the Jews in Reform congregations had no interest in creating a denomination, or separate stream, within American Judaism. They identified with all other Jews. Even if they did not know the phrase, they believed in a principle found in the Talmud: *kol yisrael arevim zeh b'zeh*, "all of the people of Israel are responsible for each other." ("Israel" here refers to the Jewish people.)

Although Jews were beginning to divide into groups according to their views about reform, they presented a united front when members of their faith faced prejudice and discrimination. Jews organized and protested to call attention to these problems. In 1840, for example, Jews in the United States, Great Britain, and France protested the actions of some Christians and Muslims in Syria who accused Jews of killing people and using the blood to make *matzo*. This kind of accusation, called a blood libel, had been common in the Middle Ages, but Jews in America and western Europe were shocked that it could happen again in the 19th century.

Another example of solidarity occurred in 1855, when Jewish communities across the United States held meetings and wrote letters on behalf of Jewish merchants who wanted to do business in Switzerland. The Swiss government did not give Jewish businessmen, even American citizens, the same rights it extended to others. Jews believed that this was wrong and wanted the United States government to break an 1850 treaty with Switzerland unless it changed its discriminatory policy, although neither happened. And in 1858, after Christians in an Italian city had kidnapped and forcibly baptized a Jewish child, leaders such as Leeser and Wise, along with American Jewish newspapers and magazines, rallied American Jews to protest.

There was no conflict between being American and being Jewish. American Jews felt that they were part of a worldwide Jewish people, but they also felt connected to the United States. They got involved in the civic affairs of their communities, something that would have been difficult in Europe. They voted, served on juries, joined volunteer fire companies, and worked in law enforcement. They held elective office, especially in small towns. Voters in Los Angeles elected Morris Goodman, a

Bavarian immigrant, to the city council in 1850, and two years later voters in San Francisco elected Elcan Heydenfeldt to the California state assembly. The people of Virgina City, Nevada, made Jewish immigrant Mark Strouse their chief of police in 1863. Bernard Goldsmith served as mayor of Portland, Oregon, from 1869 to 1871.

In Chicago, peddler-turned-shopkeeper Abraham Kohn became active in the newly formed Republican party during the 1850s. The Republican party reflected Kohn's strong aversion to slavery. His contribution to the party paid off: In 1860 he was elected city clerk. Probably because of Kohn's position and his service to the party, an important Illinois Republican, Abraham Lincoln, visited Kohn in his clothing store in 1860. We do not know what they talked about, but after Lincoln was elected President Kohn gave him a very special gift—a satin replica of the American flag that Kohn had made. It was embroidered with words from Josh. 4:9 in the Bible, in both Hebrew and English: "As I was with Moses, so I will be with thee; I will not fail thee, nor forsake thee. Be strong and of good courage."

Those last six words might have been a motto for the Jews of the United States during the mid-1800s. The years between 1820 and 1880 saw both improvement and deterioration in their condition. The last laws that allowed Jews and others to be kept out of political life because of their religion were eliminated. In 1826, after a very heated debate, the Maryland state legislature passed the "Jew Bill," which allowed Jews to hold political office. New Hampshire removed its last legal restrictions on Jews in 1877, North Carolina in 1885. Very few Jews lived in these states, however, so the exclusion of Jews from full participation in public affairs had not become a major political issue there.

Equality was now the law, but relations between Jews and the largely Protestant majority were not always smooth. Some Protestant sects believed that it was their duty to convert the Jews to Christianity. These evangelicals considered the conversion of the Jews an important step in the Christian mission to hasten the Second Coming of Christ. One such group was the American Society for Meliorating the Condition of the Jews (ASMCJ), founded in 1820 by Elias Boudinot, who had been a minor official in George Washington's administration. It and other

organizations tried to convince Jews that Judaism was wrong and Christianity right. The ASMCJ's constitution expressed its commitment to "employing missionaries to labor among the Jews of the United States, to the temporal relief of indigent and deserving individuals of that denomination, to the circulation of tracts, Bibles, and testaments among them, and to the communication of Christian instruction through any other appropriate channel." The ASMCJ set up programs to attract Jews, particularly women and children. It turned storefronts in Jewish neighborhoods into schools and recreation centers for the poor and distributed food, hoping in the process to convert the Jews. One of its tactics was to roam the charity wards of hospitals looking for Jews who were about to die, then try to get the dying people to make deathbed conversions.

In response, Jewish communities formed their own organizations. Leaders such as Isaac Leeser and Rebecca Gratz, an influential member of Leeser's Philadelphia congregation Mikveh Israel, feared the Christian missionaries and founded projects to counteract them. With Leeser's blessing, Gratz opened the first Jewish Sunday school in 1838 in Philadelphia. Before that time, parents arranged for children to receive Jewish instruction from private tutors, and some congregations had

Constitution of the United Hebrew Beneficent Society of Philadelphia

Wherever Jews settled they created institutions to provide for assistance and companionship. Even before they formed synagogues they found ways to help each other in times of crisis. They believed that they were responsible for themselves and for each other. In 1822, the Jews of Philadelphia created the United Hebrew Beneficent Society and drafted a constitution to clearly state its purpose.

PREAMBLE

To provide in the best manner possible for the relief of our unfortunate and indigent brethren, and to ameliorate their sufferings to the utmost of our abilities, is the performance of an obligation which strengthens the bonds of society, by the endearing ties of benevolence and gratitude.

Impressed with these truths, we whose names are hereto subscribed, citizens of the State of Pennsylvania, hereby united in a benevolent association, and for our government, as members thereof, adopt the following rules and regulations; each of us pledging himself to the others to observe them with honour and good faith.

schools. Gratz, however, opened her school to poor Jewish children. Leeser and Gratz picked Sunday for the school because on that day all the shops and schools were closed and children would be able to attend.

Leeser held traditional views on Jewish religious practice and thought that teachers should be men, not women. But he was willing to depart from past practices and let Gratz open her school because he considered the missionary threat so great. Gratz and Leeser hoped that the school would give the youngsters enough awareness of and pride in the Jewish tradition that they would not be swayed by the evangelicals.

Most Protestant Americans did not think that Judaism deserved the same respect as Christianity, especially Protestant Christianity. The institutions of American public life were biased toward Christianity. Like all children in public schools, Jewish children recited Christian prayers and read from the King James Version of the Bible, the standard Protestant text. Laws that required businesses to close on Sunday, the Christian day of rest, also meant that Jews could not keep their businesses open on that day—even though they observed their Sabbath on Saturday. In 1861 the Appellate Court of New York declared that Christianity was part of the state's common law, saying that although the law should respect and protect other religions, Christianity was "the acknowledged religion of the people." In 1864 Senator Charles Sumner of Pennsylvania introduced an amendment to the federal Constitution that would declare the United States a "Christian government." Congress, however, believed that it violated the fundamental intent of the Constitution's framers and did not pass the amendment.

Private institutions also reflected the bias against a non-Christian religion taking root in the United States. In 1874 Cornell University in Ithaca, New York, hired Felix Adler, a rabbi and the son of a rabbi, to teach Hebrew. Like many colleges, Cornell offered courses in Hebrew to equip scholars to study the Bible. But one magazine said of Adler's appointment, "Christianity is imperiled in consequence."

All religions enjoyed the protection and neutrality of the Constitution and the legal system. Sometimes, however, the attitudes of the Christian majority became matters of public policy—and Jews challenged it. During the Civil War, for example, about 7,000 Jewish men served in the Union Army and 3,000 Southern Jews fought for the Confederacy. In fact, Jewish men joined the armies of the Union and the

TEACHERS' AND PARENTS'

ASSISTANT;

OR,

THIRTEEN LESSONS

CONVEYING TO UNINFORMED MINDS THE FIRST IDEAS OF
GOD AND HIS ATTRIBUTES.

BY AN AMERICAN JEWESS.

PHILADELPHIA:
C. SHERMAN, PRINTER.
5605.

Rebecca Gratz opened the first Jewish Sunday school in 1838. But there were no books for Jewish children or manuals for teachers in English, so she wrote her own. This book was published in 1845 (the Jewish year 5606).

Confederacy in a somewhat higher proportion than the general population, and on the home front Jewish women raised money for the troops, sewed bandages, and provided the same kinds of support services that other women did. But in 1861 Congress declared that regiments could choose the *Christian* clergyman of their choice as chaplain and turned the army's chaplaincy program over to the Young Men's Christian Association (YMCA).

A number of Jews served in the 65th Regiment of the 5th Pennsylvania Cavalry, commanded by Colonel Max Friedman, a Jew. They elected as their chaplain Sergeant Michael Allen. Although Allen was not a rabbi, he was a Hebrew teacher who had studied in Europe to become a rabbi. When the YMCA discovered this violation of the law, it used the threat of dishonorable discharge to force Allen to resign. Undaunted, the regiment elected another Jewish chaplain—Arnold Fischel, an ordained rabbi from New York. The War Department rejected his election because Fischel was not Christian. Jews across America protested, and one rabbi wrote to Congress in support of Jewish soldiers' rights to religious freedom "according to the constitution of the U.S. which they endeavor to preserve and defend with all their might." The nation for which these soldiers were fighting surely should not insult their religion. After hearing protests and reading petitions, Congress changed the law in 1862 so that Jewish clergy could serve as chaplains.

Religious intolerance was not the only problem Jews encountered in their relations with Gentile Americans. Not only did some Gentiles consider Judaism an alien religion that did not belong in a Christian nation, they often harbored ethnic prejudices against Jews as a people. Many Americans harbored attitudes that today would be called anti-Semitic. (The terms "Semitic race" and "anti-Semitism," meaning "prejudice against Jews," appeared in Germany in 1879. It referred to Jews as "Semites," a specific racial group. This is distinct from the later term "Semitic languages," used to define the linguistic grouping of Hebrew, Arabic, Aramaic, and Amharic.)

These anti-Semitic Americans believed that Jews were fundamentally different from other people. Sometimes they even thought that Jews *looked* different, with physical features that set them apart from others. Cartoon drawings, literature, and drama depicted Jews with very large noses, deep dark eyes, and deformed bodies. These physical stereotypes were accompanied by other ideas about Jews—that they were greedy, that they loved only money, and that they felt no loyalty to the country where they lived. Such anti-Jewish attitudes were the fruit of many centuries of European history during which Christians had persecuted, mistrusted, and dehumanized the Jews.

Most Americans who held anti-Semitic views kept them to themselves, but sometimes anti-Jewish feelings became actions. On December 17, 1862, in the midst of the Civil War, General Ulysses S. Grant issued an order expelling all Jews from the military district under his command (Mississippi, Kentucky, and Tennessee). Grant claimed that Jews were making profits by trading with the Confederacy and that "Jews, as a class [were] violating every regulation of trade established by the Treasury Department."

Such things had happened to Jews before, in Europe. But the United States was different. European Jews affected by orders like Grant's had packed their bags and moved somewhere else. But the Jews of Paducah, Kentucky, knowing that the Constitution and U.S. law protected them, sent a representative to Washington to meet with President Lincoln, express their outrage, and demand a change in policy. Lincoln—perhaps remembering Abraham Kohn and the gift of the flag—immediately canceled Grant's order.

Not all problems of discrimination were so easily resolved. Joseph Seligman was a fabulously wealthy Jewish businessman in New York City. He helped the United States greatly during the Civil War by marketing Union bonds on European money markets. In 1877 Seligman set out with his entire household for a summer vacation at Saratoga Springs, an elegant resort town in upstate New York. When the Seligmans entered the Grand Union Hotel—where they had vacationed for years—the manager of the hotel refused to admit them. He told Seligman that the hotel no longer received Jewish guests. The better sort of Christians who vacationed at Saratoga Springs considered Jews vulgar and flashy and did not want to spend their leisure time with such crude types.

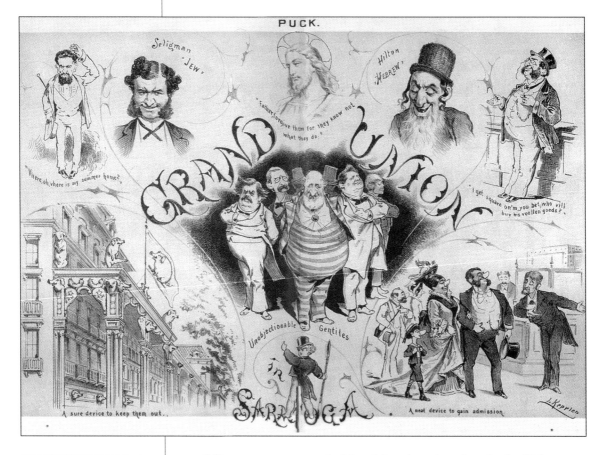

Puck, a popular American magazine of the late 19th century, satirized the behavior of the Grand Union Hotel in Saratoga Springs, New York, when it refused to accommodate its longtime customer Jacob Seligman. Jewish law prohibits eating pork, and the pigs on the front porch (left) imply the lenghts the hotel will go to in order to keep Jews out.

Seligman was not a typical Jew. Most American Jews in the 19th century could not have afforded to stay at the Grand Union Hotel. They were more like Abraham Kohn, who had started as an impoverished immigrant peddler, then owned a very small store, and finally become the proprietor of a modestly successful business. Some American Jews were quite poor; throughout this era every Jewish community had to deal with the problems of poverty. The communities considered it their moral obligation to help widows and orphans, newly arrived immigrants with no money, and the many failed peddlers who could not make it in the United States.

Between 1820 and 1880 the Jewish population in the United States rose from 4,000 to about 250,000. By 1880 Jews lived in almost every state, generally clustered in cities. A quarter of all American Jews lived in New York City.

Despite their successes, however, Jews stood on the margins of American society. At any time, from any direction, criticism and hostility could come their way. But if they still felt like outsiders in the United States, Jews nevertheless joined with other Americans in civic activities and public causes, voting, holding office, and participating in public life for the common good. They celebrated American holidays such as Thanksgiving and the Fourth of July. Their American-raised or American-born children spoke English and identified with the United States.

In 1876 Philadelphia hosted the Centennial Exposition, a fair that marked the 100th anniversary of American independence. The Jewish contribution to the exposition was provided by the B'nai B'rith, an organization that American Jews had founded in New York in 1843 for mutual support and assistance. By 1876 it had lodges all over the country. For the Exposition, the B'nai B'rith erected a statue called "Religious Liberty." Created by a Jewish sculptor named Moses Ezekiel, it symbolized what Jews held most dear about the United States—its commitment to freedom of religion.

The 19th century had seen a transformation in which Jews had changed from immigrants to Americans, adjusting themselves as much as possible to life in the United States. Yet that adjustment would soon be complicated by dramatic events in Europe.

Chapter 3

Transplanted People: 1880–1924

The American poet Emma Lazarus was descended on her father's side from Sephardim who could trace their ancestry back to Spain. Her mother's family were German Jewish immigrants who had prospered in the United States. In 1883 Lazarus entered a poetry competition. The organizers of the competition planned to auction off the winning poem to raise money for something unusual, something monumental— the pedestal on which an enormous statue would stand. The statue was of a woman holding a torch, and it was to be placed on Bedloe's Island at the tip of Manhattan in New York Harbor, the gateway to the United States.

Emma Lazarus won the competition, but the story does not have a perfectly happy ending. Lazarus died at 33, before the statue's unveiling. The plaque bearing her poem was not fastened to the statue for another 20 years—and then it somehow got placed inside the pedestal where few could see it. It would be 30 more years before the plaque was moved to the outside of the Statue of Liberty.

Neither the poetry contest nor the statue was inspired by the massive wave of immigration flowing into the United States. France had given the statue to the United States as a symbol of French-American friendship. But to Emma Lazarus—a young Jewish woman who had grown up in freedom and comfort in New York City—the United States meant the promise of a better life for people suffering elsewhere.

The image of the Statue of Liberty was the beacon of welcome to those seeking freedom and opportunity, and it played a powerful role in the words and graphic images produced by Jewish immigrants and millions of others.

Between 1880 and 1924, about 30 million immigrants, such as these men at Ellis Island, arrived in the United States from Europe, primarily from eastern and southern regions. Of those, 2.5 million were Jews who came primarily from Russia, Poland, and parts of the Austro-Hungarian Empire.

The more than 25 million immigrants who arrived in the United States between 1880 and 1924 could not read Lazarus's words, but her poem, "The New Colossus," was about their experiences. In particular, it expressed the feelings of 2.5 million eastern European Jewish immigrants, most of whom entered the United States through New York Harbor, passing beneath the "Mother of Exiles," as Lazarus called the statue. She wrote:

> Give me your tired, your poor,
> Your huddled masses yearning to breathe free,
> The wretched refuse of your teeming shore,
> Send these, the homeless, tempest-tost to me,
> I lift my lamp beside the golden door!

To millions of Jews in eastern Europe, the chance to come to the United States represented a golden opportunity. Their letters, folk sayings, and music called the United States Columbus's *goldene medine*, "golden land." They did not expect to find riches effortlessly in the United States, but they saw the country as a place where they could make a living—and a place where they could *live.*

Survival weighed heavily on their minds. Life had never been comfortable for eastern European Jews. Some lived in Russia, under the rule of the czars. Others lived in Poland, which became an independent country in 1920 (for several centuries before that it had been divided among Germany, Russia, and Austria-Hungary). Millions more lived in Romania and the eastern provinces of Austria-Hungary. Eastern European Jews had few rights, sometimes none. In Russia, they could not live outside a part of the country called the Pale. Everywhere laws set limits on where Jews could travel and what jobs they could hold.

For centuries Jews had occupied a particular role in the economy: traders, peddlers, middlemen between the upper classes and the vast majority of peasants. Jews also worked as artisans, innkeepers, and liquor distillers. After about 1860, however, relations between peasants and landowners and between city and country people changed. Because of the coming of the railroad, the beginnings of factory production, the emancipation of the serfs, and urban development, eastern Europe did not need the Jews and their traditional occupations any longer. The Jews faced increasing poverty. To escape it, many moved to the cities of eastern Europe and took jobs in new factories, particularly clothing factories. But there were too few factories to absorb the Jews who had been displaced. Millions could not make a living in either the cities or the *shtetlach*, the small Jewish towns. Some faced starvation. Few believed that they had a future in Europe.

It was not just that they could not make a living. Relations between the Jews and the Gentiles had long been tense, and from time to time Jews had been the victims of acts of violence. But after 1881 the violence was organized, systematic, and tolerated—maybe even encouraged—by governments, especially in Russia. Pogroms, organized attacks on Jewish communities, were bloody and frequent. Not only did the authorities not defend the Jews, they often helped cause the pogroms. Jews were robbed, beaten, raped, and killed. Rioters destroyed their homes, looted their stores, and burned their synagogues. In 1881 and 1882, a total of 225 Jewish communities endured pogroms.

The violence continued, with brief lulls between outbreaks. So many pogroms broke out in 1906 that Jewish leaders admitted that they could not keep track of the number. That year 800 Jews died in a pogrom in the city of Odessa alone. Pogroms were likely to occur when Gentiles faced economic or political hard times. The peasants took out their anger and frustration on the Jews, who had long been the scapegoats for European Christians.

Some of the worst pogroms followed a failed Russian revolution in 1905 and Russia's defeat in the Russo-Japanese War the following year. Violence against Jews was also severe from 1914 through the early 1920s, years that saw World War I in Europe and the Communist Revolution in Russia.

Those who could escape fled to the United States. About a third of all eastern European Jews emigrated to the United States between 1880 and 1924. Jewish immigration averaged 20,000 a year from 1881 to 1892 and 37,000 a year from 1892 to 1903. Between 1903 and the start of World War I in 1914, when immigration ground to a halt, 76,000 eastern European Jews came to the United States.

That number could have been higher, but some Jews went to Canada, Argentina, Australia, or South Africa because they could not meet the requirements for admission to the United States. Those requirements were spelled out in immigration laws that the U.S. Congress passed in 1891, 1903, 1907, and 1917. The immigration laws prevented certain kinds of people from entering the United States. Most restrictions involved people with diseases such as tuberculosis and trachoma. Others were aimed at keeping out the extremely poor, whom Congress feared would be an expense to the public.

In 1924, however, Congress closed the doors of the United States to the flood of immigrants eager to enter the country. It passed the Johnson Act, a law that created quotas for immigration. Each country in the world was assigned a specific number, and only that many people from that country could emigrate to the United States each year. The countries where most Jews lived, such as Russia and Poland, received very low quotas, which meant that few immigrants from these lands could enter.

Although the Johnson Act cut the flow of Jewish immigrants to a trickle, immigration had already brought tremendous changes to Jewish life in America. By 1925 4.5 million Jews lived in the United States, which had one of the world's largest Jewish populations. Jews were still a minority in the country, but their numbers had grown enormously.

The Jewish migration was different from the migrations of many other ethnic groups. In most cases, more men than women came to the United States. Among Italians, Greeks, Poles, and Hungarians, for example, male immigrants outnumbered female immigrants because many of the men planned to return to their homelands after earning money in the United States. They did not bring their families with them, although over time many decided to stay in their new homeland and sent for their wives and other relatives.

But Jewish women, like their brothers, wanted to get out of Europe. Women and men alike intended to make a new start in the United States, and they immigrated in equal numbers. In large American cities—particularly New York, where almost three-quarters of them settled—the Jewish immigrants married, had children, and established new communities. They had come to stay.

In other ways, though, the Jewish immigrants from eastern Europe were much like other immigrant groups. Most were young, between the ages of 16 and 45. These able-bodied workers, both men and women, found jobs and worked not just to make a living for themselves but also to bring over other family members. The majority of them went to work in garment factories. Most of the others opened small shops. Many who started out as factory workers later opened stores and became self-employed, although on a small scale.

In the 1880s conditions deteriorated for the millions of Jews who lived in czarist Russia. They not only endured increasing poverty and economic displacement but the regime imposed harsh edicts upon them, including mass expulsions from towns and regions.

Most of the Jewish immigrants were young men and women who rightly believed that they had no future in Russia and other parts of eastern Europe. One important part of starting a new life was getting married, and Jewish communities in America celebrated weddings with style, even if both bride and groom labored in factories.

A quarter of the Jewish immigrants, however, were younger than 16 or older than 45. The Jewish immigration included young children and older people because whole Jewish communities uprooted themselves and transplanted themselves to the United States. They had to think about educating their children for life in the United States as well as life in a Jewish community.

Their experiences before immigration shaped the communities they built in the United States. Like all immigrants, they had unique cultural traditions, many of which remained unchanged in their new homes. Other traditions, however, would change dramatically as people adapted to American conditions.

In eastern Europe, Jews lived in dense, all-Jewish communities. Particularly in small towns, life revolved around traditional practices. People observed Jewish law in every part of their lives, and Jewish values underlay everything they did. They revered the rabbis and scholars who studied Jewish law. Those rabbis warned the Jews of eastern Europe against going to the United States. The rabbis feared that Jews who wished to observe their traditions would find life difficult in the United

States, which one rabbi called a *"trefa medinah,"* an unclean land. No doubt the rabbis were aware of the rise of Reform Judaism in the United States and of the general relaxation of piety there. Perhaps they even knew that in 1885 a conference of Reform rabbis in Pittsburgh had passed a Declaration of Principles that dramatically altered what it meant to be a Jew. The American Reform rabbis had declared that "all such . . . laws as regulate diet" are no longer necessary. They had also announced, "We consider ourselves no longer a nation but a religious community." To traditional Jews in eastern Europe these changes conflicted with a basic principle of traditional Judaism: that God, Torah, and the people Israel represented a single, unbreakable unity. Judaism, to traditional Jews, did not separate religion from the idea of peoplehood. It also did not give anyone the right to invalidate laws considered divinely ordained.

The rabbis who did not want Jews to go to the United States also knew how hard Jews there worked to make a living, often violating the Sabbath and ignoring other elements of tradition to support their families. No matter what the rabbis said, however, life had become perilously difficult for Jews in eastern Europe. The shadow of the pogroms hung over them. Vast numbers of them enthusiastically left for the United States, where they searched for ways to be true to tradition while making a new life for themselves.

They created religious institutions that reflected their love of tradition. Dozens of kosher butcher shops and bakeries sprang up in Jewish neighborhoods. So did small schools modeled on the eastern European *heder* (a school that taught young children Hebrew language, prayer, and the basics of the Bible and some Talmud). Communities also built *mikvaot,* or places for ritual bathing, so that men and women could conform to the rules of family purity, which required married couples to refrain from sexual contact during and for a week after the wife's menstrual period; at the end of this time, the wife would immerse herself in a *mikvah.*

In their neighborhoods the Jews organized small congregations, usually made up of men who came from the same small

Food merchants were among the most important figures in any city. Respected members of the community often advertised their grocery businesses with the title Dr. after their names, as Moritz Kohn did on this sales statement.

Jews had special dietary needs because of the laws of *kashrut*, which regulated the Jewish diet. Consumers would want to know that the meat they bought conformed to those rules and that shopowners, such as this couple, followed the strict kosher procedures.

towns, cities, or regions in eastern Europe. Known as *hevrot* (informal groups) or *anshes* ("men of," followed by the name of the town), these groups prayed as they had back home. Often they met in storefronts or the basements of apartment buildings—very different from the large, majestic synagogues that were being built by Jews who had been in the United States for a long time.

Some of the more prosperous eastern European immigrants formed new, more elaborate Orthodox congregations or joined older traditional ones. The first Russian synagogue in New York, Congregation Beth Hamedrash, was founded in 1852. In 1872 it adopted the name Kahal Adath Jeshurun Anshe Lubtz, "the congregation of the community of Jeshurun, the people of the town of Lubtz." In 1887, as new arrivals from eastern Europe made their way to the Lower East Side every day, the synagogue dedicated an ornate building on Eldridge Street in the heart of that neighborhood. The Eldridge Street Synagogue symbolized the upward mobility of the immigrants, who prayed in a traditional style and observed the details of Jewish practice.

Some young immigrant men studied at the Jewish Theological Seminary of America (JTS), a New York City–based training school for rabbis. JTS had been founded in 1886 by wealthy Jews, most of whom had been born in the United States or had lived there for a long time. It began as an Orthodox, but American, seminary. During the 1910s and 1920s, JTS would gradually create Conservative Judaism, a form of Judaism midway between Orthodoxy and Reform.

In its early decades, however, JTS tried to build a bridge between eastern European Orthodoxy and American life. Its founders feared that the American-born children of eastern European immigrants would be drawn to neither the old-style Orthodoxy from Russia and Poland nor the formality and churchlike decorum of Reform. The founders of JTS wanted the school to be American in its outward style while remaining true to the core of traditional Jewish practice. One of its earliest students was Mordecai Kaplan, a young immigrant from Lithuania, who would later play a crucial role in defining and shaping American Judaism.

Like the JTS, the Rabbi Itzhak Elhanan Theological Seminary (RIETS) wanted to train Orthodox rabbis who were both deeply committed to tradition and at home in the United States. RIETS opened in New York City in 1915; in 1928 it became the nucleus of Yeshiva University. Yet RIETS traced its origins to the 1880s, when Jews in New York had founded two *yeshivas,* or Hebrew schools: Etz Chaim ("tree of life") and Mahzike Talmud Torah ("those who hold on to the study of the Torah"). The founders of these Orthodox schools had tried to create in the United States traditional institutions just like those of eastern Europe—but this was not possible. Even the most committed traditional institutions had to add secular American studies, and the young men who studied in them soon adopted American ways.

Jews in the United States found the issue of religious authority vexing. In Europe rabbis received power

Immigrant Jews from eastern Europe, like those in Boston's West End, built their own synagogues rather than attend those founded by the well-established American Jews. This congregation, Tifereth Israel, represented the steady economic advancement of the immigrants.

Rabbi Jacob Joseph, a great scholar from Lithuania, was invited to New York in the 1880s by a group of orthodox congregations. They believed that American Jews needed a chief rabbi to bring order to the chaos of ritual practice, education, and charity. But American Jews liked American-style democracy and the office of the chief rabbi was quickly dismantled.

from two sources. First, the masses of Jews accepted their pronouncements and obeyed their rules. Second, the state governments gave the rabbis authority over civil matters in Jewish communities. For example, since the mid-19th century Great Britain had had a Chief Rabbi who could, and did, make rules that *all* Jewish congregations in Britain had to follow. The British government recognized his authority.

But the United States was different. The Constitution forbade Congress from interfering in religion, and religious leaders had authority only by the voluntary consent of church members. Jews, Christians, and followers of any other faith had every right to start their own congregations, write their own rules, or create new practices.

Some American Jews, however, felt a need for greater authority. In 1888 several Orthodox congregations in New York decided to bring Rabbi Jacob Joseph from Lithuania to run New York's Orthodox community—to become "chief rabbi" of the city. Joseph was an impressive speaker and a respected Talmudic scholar. His sponsors hoped that he would recreate some of the religious authority that governed Jewish life in Europe. They wanted him to organize the *shochtim* and kosher butchers to regulate the kosher meat industry in New York; to establish rabbinic courts like those that ruled Jewish communities in eastern Europe; and to supervise Jewish education and charities. But even among the Orthodox, very few American Jews accepted Jacob Joseph's authority. American society—with its separation of church and state and its emphasis on liberty and individuality—made it impossible for the idea of a "chief rabbi" to flourish.

Politics also shaped the lives of the eastern European immigrants. Many of them came from industrial cities where they had learned about new ideas that challenged the old-style traditionalism of the *shtetlach*. Among these new political philosophies was Marxism, which questioned the morality of an economic system in which workers labored many hours under horrible conditions, lived poorly, and earned paltry salaries while owners enjoyed a life of luxury. Many young Jewish women and men joined labor unions and other organizations like the Bund (the General Jewish Workers' Union in Lithuania, Poland, and Russia, founded in 1897 in Russia) to try to change society. They struggled to give workers greater rights, better pay, and decent working conditions. Some of them dreamed of a future society based on socialism, a political and economic system in which the state, rather than private owners, would own and operate factories and farms.

Jewish immigrants from eastern Europe brought socialist ideas to the United States. They settled in New York, Chicago, Philadelphia, Boston, Baltimore, and other large cities and went to work in garment factories. And they challenged the American idea that workers had no right to organize. In 1900 Jews who sewed men's clothing organized the Amalgamated Clothing Workers' Union. In 1914 Jewish and Italian laborers who made women's clothing founded the International Ladies' Garment Workers' Union (ILGWU). Furriers, hat makers, bakers, printers, and others also contributed to a large Jewish labor movement in the United States.

Many members of the labor movement considered themselves socialists and wanted to bring their philosophy of "share the wealth" to American politics. In 1886 the Jewish Workingmen's Association linked itself with the Socialist Labor party. In 1914 the Lower East Side, New York's densest Jewish neighborhood, elected a socialist named Meyer London to Congress.

Even when immigrant Jews did not join socialist organizations or vote for socialist candidates, socialist ideas affected their culture. The Jewish immigrants tended to be politically active. They voted in large numbers—a privilege they cherished because in their former homelands they had had no voice in politics. And they tended to vote for liberal candidates, those who wanted to expand the role of government in social programs such as helping the poor. After all, the immigrants arrived in the United States during the Progressive Era, a period when reformers challenged old ideas about government. Instead of simply letting society continue as it had been, reformers believed that it was government's

MOORE THEATRE

מור טעאַטער

By special request of the Yid-
dish Public of Seattle. The cel-
ebrated Yiddish Prima Donna
Madam Regina Prager and her
Company will give 2 Special
Performances.
Tuesday, April 2

HADASSA הדסה

1912

פרייען ליעבע

WOMEN LOVE

$1.50 און $1.00 .ס 75 .ס 50 .ס 35 :פרייזען פיר פלעטצער

Tickets Now on Sale at Box Office

The Yiddish actress and
singer Regina Prager and
her company toured Amer-
ican Jewish communities in
1912. Eastern European
immigrants enjoyed going
to the theater to hear
Yiddish songs and see
Jewish plays.

responsibility to regulate the economy, protect workers, ensure a decent living for all,
and help the unfortunate.

Jews sided with the progressive element in
American politics partly because many of
them were poor and faced hardships. In New
York and other cities they lived in dilapidated,
unsafe housing, with many people to a room.
Their houses stood on streets piled high with
uncollected garbage. These conditions bred
infectious diseases, especially tuberculosis.

Immigrants tried to solve their own problems, turning first to family for assistance.
Many families formed clubs. Besides being
places to have a good time and celebrate holidays and events such as weddings, these clubs
were a way for members to provide each other
with interest-free loans. Such loans, called *gemilass chesed* ("acts of loving
kindness"), grew out of traditional Jewish practice.

The immigrants also formed *landsmanshaften,* associations of people
from the same town or area in Europe. These organizations provided
members with insurance benefits, the services of a doctor, and burials.
Immigrants may have joined the *landsmanshaften* for social reasons, but
in times of crisis the organizations tried to take the place of the tight, sup-
portive communities that Jews had known in Europe.

Not all Jews in the United States struggled. Some of them—especially
some of those who had been in the country for a long time—earned
comfortable livings as merchants. A few bankers and financiers were
extremely wealthy. These prosperous Jews felt some responbility toward
the newly arrived immigrants—and also a bit of embarrassment at the
arrival of so many poor, Yiddish-speaking Jews from eastern Europe. The
wealthy American Jews wanted to ease the poverty of the new immigrants
and help them adjust to the United States. In 1893 a group of Jewish philanthropists created the Educational Alliance on New York's Lower East

Side. For children, the Educational Alliance provided religious education; for adults it offered classes in practical skills such as stenography, typewriting, and bookkeeping. It even taught people how to take the U.S. Civil Service examinations so that they could qualify for government jobs. The Educational Alliance also offered English classes, so that the immigrants could learn the language of their adopted country, and a Legal Aid Bureau to help them with legal problems.

Another organization founded in 1893 was the National Council of Jewish Women. One of its members, Lizzie Black Kander, wanted to do something for the eastern European Jewish women who had settled in Milwaukee. In 1896 she opened the Milwaukee Jewish Mission. It was a settlement house, a community center in the heart of a poor neighborhood; other settlement houses had appeared in American cities in the late 1800s. Kander decided that the immigrant women should learn how to cook like Americans. She thought that their eastern European diet lacked nutritional value. So she wrote a cookbook for them. *The Settlement Cookbook* appeared as a pamphlet in Yiddish in 1901. It went on to become one of the best-selling American cookbooks, used by people of many backgrounds over many years.

One of the small group of very wealthy Jewish financiers was Jacob Schiff, who lived in New York. Schiff believed that the biggest problem faced by the Jewish immigrants was that too many of them had chosen to settle in New York. Schiff came up with the "Galveston Plan" to divert Jewish immigrants from New York and send them to Texas. He thought that by going to Galveston and then spreading out to other parts of the unsettled Southwest, Jews would avoid the unhealthy, overcrowded neighborhoods of the big cities. They could be farmers rather than garment workers. In 1907 he created the Jewish Immigrants Information Bureau to help find work for those who went to Galveston.

Boys and girls at Congregation B'nai Israel in Galveston, Texas, went through the new ritual of confirmation in the 1890s. Girls had traditionally never participated in any kind of public, coming-of-age ceremony, but confirmation, a practice in Reform congregations, recognized the formal completion of their Jewish schooling.

Perhaps Schiff had a good idea, but it never amounted to much. However desperate the conditions of the Jews in New York and the other cities, immigrants continued to flock to the big cities. New York was the single largest Jewish community. Almost 45 percent of American Jews lived there in 1927. The next largest concentration was Chicago, with 8 percent of American Jews. The difference between those two figures shows how much Jewish life was centered on New York. Yet Philadelphia, Boston, Cleveland, and Detroit had sizable Jewish communities as well.

Some Jews did move out of the big cities of the Northeast and the Midwest. A few eastern European Jews, like the central Europeans before them, tried to make a living by peddling. Like the Jews who had come earlier in the century, they peddled for a few years in the country-side and then settled down in towns and small cities like Kansas City, Missouri; Norfolk, Virginia; Portland, Oregon; Denver, Colorado; or Houston, Texas.

An even smaller number tried their luck at farming in the rural areas of New York and New Jersey as well as in Nebraska, Iowa, and Washington State. But they had little knowledge of agriculture, and most of them had a hard time. They faced the insecurities of weather and market prices that all American farmers faced, and they lacked the comfort of a Jewish community. One Jewish farm wife left a touching record of her distress. Rachel Kahn came from Russia in 1894, traveling alone to marry Abraham Calof. She had never even met Calof, but with few opportunities for work or marriage in Russia she took the chance of marrying a man she did not know and going to a strange new land. She spent most of the rest of her life on a homestead in North Dakota. In her memoir she wrote of the loneliness and disorientation she felt there:

> Dear God, I thought, whatever your reason, haven't I suffered enough. . . . The people, the overwhelming prairie, America itself, seemed strange and terrible. I had no place to turn. There were no other homes to be seen on the vast expanse of the great plain. . . . Despair gave birth to courage. Thank God. I would have great need of it before long.

Whether on farms, in small towns, or in big industrial cities, all of the immigrants needed courage. The crises of their time went far beyond

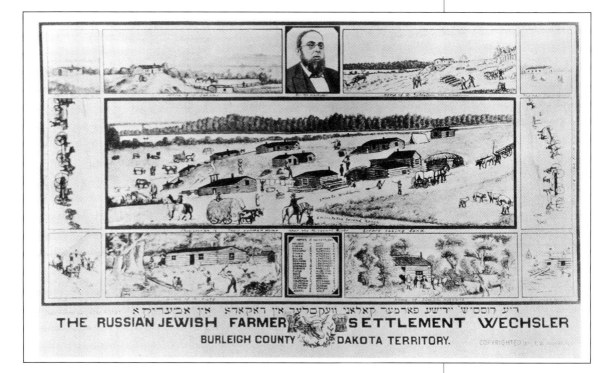

THE RUSSIAN JEWISH FARMER SETTLEMENT WECHSLER
BURLEIGH COUNTY DAKOTA TERRITORY.

individual problems. To survive, they would need more than the goodwill of philanthropists.

The Jewish immigrants of the late 19th and early 20th centuries faced the difficulties endured by all of America's poor. They suffered like all workers who labored in an industrial society that offered them no protection. Factory owners not only paid them low wages but also made them work long hours in unsafe working conditions. The *landsmanshaften*, family clubs, and synagogues could not protect them here.

A tragedy that called the nation's attention to the suffering of laborers took the lives of many young Jewish women. In 1911 a fire broke out in the Asch Building in New York City. The Triangle Shirt Waist Company, a manufacturer of women's clothing, had its workrooms in the building. The fire claimed the lives of 140 workers, almost all young Jewish women from immigrant families, because the factory owner had locked the door from the outside and the building had inadequate fire escapes. The trapped workers had no way out.

Dr. Judah Wechsler attempted to attract Russian Jews to farming colonies in the American Midwest. In 1865 he began publishing a newspaper called *The Russian Jewish Farmer*. In that same year he founded an unsuccessful colony in the Dakota Territory. Most Jewish immigrants had no interest or experience in farming. They preferred the big cities.

Jewish women played a powerful role in the union-ization of the men's garment industry, helping to found and sustain the Amalgamated Clothing Workers. In the field of women's clothing they made the International Ladies' Garment Workers Union a defender of the rights of workers to demand a fair wage and tolerable working conditions.

A young woman named Fannia Cohn lived near the Asch Building and worked in a garment factory. Later she became one of the most important leaders of the ILGWU and the first woman to sit on the union's executive board. She recalled that tragedy of 1911 shaped her political attitudes. "It was the Triangle fire," she wrote "that decided my life's course."

The Triangle fire created a great deal of support for union organizing in the women's clothing industry. It also shocked American reformers, who demanded that states pass laws regulating working conditions in fac-tories and appoint inspectors to ensure that factory owners obeyed the regulations.

Socialism and labor activism reflected people's attitudes toward gov-ernment and community, and to some extent they grew out of a Jewish consciousness. But many of the immigrant Jews who identified with these political movements distanced themselves from Judaism as a religious system. They believed that Jewishness involved a sense of community and a connection to a culture but did not have to be linked to religious practice.

People who felt this way were secularists, emphasizing the nonreligious aspects of life. They considered themselves Jews but did not attend religious services, observe holidays, mark the Sabbath, or maintain a kosher diet. Some of them even wanted to liberate Jews from religious practice. A few Jewish radical secularists even went so far as to organize dances on Yom Kippur, the holy Day of Atonement that traditional Jews marked by fasting and praying for repentance. The secularists wanted to show that they had moved far beyond what they saw as the narrowness and superstition of religion.

The secular radical Jews created schools and summer camps for children to convey the message that Jewishness as a culture could be separate from Judaism as a religious system. They taught children about Jewish holidays in nonreligious terms. For example, instead of regarding Passover as the spring holiday that traditionally marks God's deliverance of the Jews from slavery in Egypt, the secularists taught that Passover commemorated the rebellion of the slaves against the oppression of the Egyptian ruling class. In 1918 secular Jews in New York created the Shalom Aleichem Folk Schools, a network of Yiddish-language schools that emphasized Jewish folk culture instead of religion. Named for a great Yiddish writer who had died two years earlier, these schools and those of the Arbeiter Ring (Workman's Circle) provided another way for Jews to live together as Jews.

The secular Jewish culture revolved around the Yiddish language. In 19th-century eastern Europe, novelists, playwrights, poets, journalists, and essayists began to produce a vast Yiddish literature. The immigrants who came to the United States strongly identified with that literature and its language.

A newspaper called *Der Forverts* (The Jewish Daily Forward) played an important role in spreading secular Jewish culture. A Russian immigrant named Abraham Cahan published the first edition of the paper on April 22, 1897, and edited it until 1946. In 1915, at the height of its

Letter to Der Forverts, *1908*

Der Forverts (Jewish Daily Forward) was the largest circulating Yiddish newspaper in the United States. It helped its readers, mostly immigrants and their children, learn about the United States and keep up with Jewish news from around the world. A popular column, "the bintel brief," or the bundle of letters, let readers write about their personal problems, and the editor, Abraham Cahan, answered in a straightforward manner.

Worthy Editor,

Have pity on me and my two small children and print my letter in the *Forward*. Max! The children and I now say farewell to you. You left us in such a terrible state. You had no compassion for us. For six years I loved you faithfully, took care of you like a loyal servant, never had a happy day with you. Yet I forgive you for everything.

Have you ever asked yourself why you left us? Max, where is your conscience: you used to have sympathy for the forsaken women and used to say their terrible plight was due to the men who left them in dire need. And how did you act? I was a young, educated, decent girl when you took me. You lived with me for six years, during which time I bore you four children. And then you left me.

Of the four children, only two remain, but you have made them living orphans. Who will bring them up? Who will support us? Have you no pity for your own flesh and blood? Consider what you are doing. My tears choke me and I cannot write any more.

Be advised that in several days I am leaving with my two living orphans for Russia. We say farewell to you and beg you to take pity on us and send us enough to live on. My address in Russia will be _____ [Full name and address were given].

Your Deserted Wife and Children

influence, the *Forverts* sold 150,000 copies a day in New York, ran special daily editions for Philadelphia, Boston, and Chicago, and even had readers in Europe. Cahan helped establish New York as the world center of Yiddish literature, especially Yiddish theater. In 1927 the *Forverts* tried to reach out to American Jews through the newest technology—radio—by sponsoring a Yiddish radio station called WEVD. The letters referred to Eugene Victor Debs, the leader of the Socialist party of the United States.

The *Forverts* and other institutions of Yiddish culture served two purposes. On one hand the schools, camps, newspapers, theaters, and clubs tried to help the immigrants become Americans. They taught the history and way of life of the United States. In the Yiddish newspapers Jewish immigrants could read about American politics and sports, as well as matters of international importance. For example, the Yiddish press wrote in tremendous detail about race relations in the United States and offered many editorials on the evils of segregation and discrimination against black people. In June 1927, an editorial in the *Forverts* condemned racism as a violation of the American tradition of equality:

> Where is the spirit of freedom with which our America is always priding itself? And where is the holiness of the Constitution which is so often mentioned. . . . Monday, the 30th of May, the American people decorated the graves of those who fell in the great battle to free the slaves in America and to free America from the stain of the shame of slavery. The slaves are today not free and on America, the stain of the shame of slavery is still evident.

On the other hand, the Yiddish newspapers and schools and other Jewish institutions wanted to ensure that the immigrants—and, more important, their children—remained committed to their Jewish past. The children of immigrants were very much drawn to the United States and American culture. In 1917, for example, 277,000 Jewish children studied in the public schools of New York while only 1,000 attended the three all-day Orthodox schools. Almost all Jewish children in New York received an education in the public schools, but only about one-fourth of them received any formal Jewish education.

Many Yiddish novels and plays dealt with the problems of immigrant adjustment. They spoke of how the authentic Jewish culture was

Der Forverts, known in English as the Jewish Daily Forward, was one of the widest-circulating foreign-language newspapers in America. In 1916 this New York–based newspaper with its socialist orientation had a daily circulation of more than 150,000, and it ran editions for Yiddish readers in a number of other U.S. cities.

lost when traditional, small-town eastern European Jews came to the United States. Abraham Cahan, the editor of the *Forverts,* wrote a novel that illustrated the dilemma of the Jewish immigrants of this period. *The Rise of David Levinsky* (1917) is the story of a devoted Talmud student who begins his journey from Europe mindful of Jewish law. He will not eat forbidden food. He prays three times a day and before every meal. Of course he observes the restrictions of the Sabbath.

Once in the United States, however, the pious young immigrant gradually casts off these practices. He cuts off his long, curly earlocks (earlocks are the mark of a pious man, based on the biblical injunction against cutting off the edges of one's hair) and he shaves (forbidden by Jewish law). He stops going to synagogue to pray but rushes off to night school to study secular subjects. At the novel's end, the miserable Levinsky speculates on what he gave up to "make it" in the United States:

> My past and my present do not comport well. David, the poor lad swinging over a Talmud volume at the Preacher's Synagogue, seems to have more in common with my inner identity than David Levinsky, the well-known cloak manufacturer.

How could American Jews balance that "past" and "present," the "inner identity" and the "outer" one? How could they be loyal both to Jewish culture and to American culture? Many American Jewish thinkers of the late 19th and early 20th centuries pondered this question. They worried that the children of immigrants were becoming *too* American.

American popular culture exerted a powerful pull on the immigrants and especially their children. Movies were tremendously appealing. By 1908 more than 400 theaters in New York City showed motion pictures. Many of those movies had been produced and written by Jews.

Moviemaking began at the same time that immigration from eastern Europe was in full swing. Early on, enterprising young Jewish immigrant men got involved in the movie industry, first by operating small movie houses in big cities. Because the motion picture industry was so new, there were no barriers to prevent newcomers from succeeding at it, and it did not take much money to get started in moviemaking. Jews became studio owners, producers, and distributors of films. At first movies were made in New York, but in the 1920s moviemaking shifted to Hollywood. The Jewish "movie moguls," as they were called, went off to California to create one of America's biggest industries. Among them was Louis B. Mayer, who left Russia as a very young child in the 1880s. By 1924 he had formed Metro-Goldwyn-Mayer (MGM), one of the world's largest

Almost all American Jews, regardless of the level of their piety or observance, flocked to religious services for the fall holidays of Rosh Hashanah and Yom Kippur. Services were held in rented halls, movie theaters, or any kind of space that could hold large crowds in order to accommodate those Jews who did not belong to synagogues.

motion picture companies. It and other studios employed many Jewish directors and screenwriters.

Ironically, the Jewish-owned film companies made very few movies about Jewish subjects. Some of their early movies, however, such as *Abie's Irish Rose* and *The Jazz Singer,* tried to encourage the Americanization of the immigrants by showing happy intermarriages between Jews and non-Jews. Their message was that "Old World" differences no longer mattered in the United States.

Popular music was another feature of American life that appealed to immigrant Jews and particularly their children. Much of that music was written in New York, by companies with offices and studios in the Flatiron Building, nicknamed "Tin Pan Alley" because of the sound of pianists banging out their tunes on all the floors. This mass-produced music was first distributed as sheet music and then recorded on phonograph records. Much of it was written or sung by Jews. Eddie Cantor, Al Jolson, Sophie Tucker, Gus Kahn, and George and Ira Gershwin wrote and performed songs that millions of Americans enjoyed.

The career of Irving Berlin illustrates the way in which Jewish tradition sometimes got lost in America. Born Israel Baline, Berlin came to the United States from Russia in 1893 at the age of five. He published his first song for Tin Pan Alley in 1907. In 1911 he wrote his first really big hit, "Alexander's Ragtime Band." Berlin wrote more than a thousand songs, including one that almost instantly became a classic hymn of American nationalism and pride, "God Bless America" (1939). Along the way, Irving Berlin ceased to be a Jew. He married a Gentile woman. His children grew up as Christians, and he wrote for them two of America's most beloved Christian songs, "White Christmas" and "Easter Parade."

Jews looked for ways to reconcile the attractions of the United States with Jewish tradition. Some thought that the answer for Jews was to remain strictly loyal to traditional Jewish teachings. This Orthodox group, however, remained a minority with little impact on the larger Jewish population. Others wanted to change the forms of Judaism to make it more like American culture—but still rooted in Jewish culture, unlike the Reform approach. People associated with the Jewish

Theological Seminary (JTS) fell into this category, but their changes occurred very slowly.

Mordecai Kaplan, a Lithuanian immigrant who was one of the early graduates of the JTS, came to the conclusion in the 1910s that Judaism in the United States had to rebuild itself, incorporating the best from tradition and American culture. In 1922, as a rabbi, Kaplan formed the Society for the Advancement of Judaism (SAJ). SAJ members experimented with religious services that retained elements of tradition and at the same time created new rituals. For example, Kaplan changed the words to the Yom Kippur prayer "Kol Nidre," because he thought it offensive to non-Jews. He also removed references in prayers to the Jews as God's "chosen people."

Some Jews looked to another part of the world for solutions to the problems of being Jewish in modern society. Young Jews in eastern Europe had begun to question the notion that Jews could live productively and peacefully among a Christian majority. They wanted to create Jewish settlements and ultimately a homeland in Palestine, as the ancient land of Israel was now called. They took the name Zionists from Zion, another name for Israel, and they created organizations, political parties, and magazines to spread the idea that Jews needed a country of their own.

Many of the Jewish immigrants who came to the United States between 1880 and 1924 sympathized with the Zionists and had belonged to Zionist organizations in Europe. They formed youth groups and adult organizations to advance the Zionist cause in the United States. One of them was Golda Mabovitch, who came to Milwaukee from the Russian city of Kiev in 1906, when she was eight years old. As a small child in Russia she had witnessed a pogrom, and she never forgot the fear and the helplessness of being a Jew in someone else's country. In 1915 she joined the Poale Zion (Labor Zionists) in Milwaukee, and in 1921 she moved to an agricultural settlement in Palestine. Many years later, in 1969, using

Irving Berlin, born in Russia as Israel Balin, wrote some of America's most popular songs, including "God Bless America." He had little formal training in music, but his sheer talent made him a successful songwriter.

The Wanderer finds Liberty in America

As a young immigrant girl in Milwaukee, Golda Meir portrayed the Statue of Liberty in a school pageant that dramatized the welcome the immigrants felt in their new American home. She grew up to become the prime minister of Israel.

the name Golda Meir, she became the fourth prime minister of the new state of Israel.

She was not typical. Most American Jews—even most Zionists—did not move to Palestine. They were grateful that the United States existed as a place of refuge, and they embraced the ideals and symbols of their new land. By and large they did well. The children of garment workers and petty merchants became high school and college graduates who entered the professions and higher levels of business. By the 1920s many young Jewish women were becoming schoolteachers, leading their families into the middle class.

Despite their success, the Jews knew that not all Americans welcomed them. Many well-off American Gentiles resented them and their achievements. Elite Americans wanted to make it impossible, or at least difficult, for Jews to attend private universities. For example, in 1922 A. Lawrence Lowell, the president of Harvard University, expressed concern that the school would become a "new Jerusalem" and started a policy that limited

Jewish enrollment to 10 percent of the student body. The presidents and trustees of many private American universities feared that their schools would become "too Jewish" unless they did something to stop the entry of Jews.

The Jews who did attend schools like Harvard, Yale, Princeton, and Columbia met stiff discrimination from the social clubs that formed the core of extracurricular life. These clubs excluded Jews from membership and made Jewish students feel uncomfortable on campus. Hardly any Jews taught in American colleges and universities. Regardless of their qualifications, Jews could not expect to find jobs as professors.

Gentiles created barriers for Jewish doctors who sought to practice in certain hospitals. Many law firms refused to hire Jewish attorneys. Even nonelite institutions like the telephone company would not employ Jewish operators.

The exclusion of Jews reached up to the highest places in American society. In 1916 President Woodrow Wilson appointed a Jew named Louis Brandeis to the U.S. Supreme Court. Brandeis had graduated from Harvard Law School in 1876. As a lawyer he had become well known for supporting the rights of ordinary people. Many Americans called him "the People's Attorney" because he took on cases to protect consumers, taxpayers, and others who felt threatened by large corporations. When he argued cases before courts he contended that policies should be evaluated by their effect on society as well as their constitutionality. This kind of argument became known as a "Brandeis brief."

Wilson, who had consulted with Brandeis on legislation that would reform American society, trusted Brandeis's judgment. But many American jurists protested his appointment of Brandeis, considering it inappropriate for a Jew to sit on the U.S. Supreme Court. The Senate deliberated the appointment for almost five months. One critic, the nephew of Massachusetts senator Henry Cabot Lodge, wrote to the Senate that Brandeis "is a Hebrew, and therefore, of Oriental race and his mind is an Oriental mind, and I think it very probable that some of his ideas . . . might not be the same as those of a man possessing an Anglo-Saxon mind." Brandeis's appointment only narrowly passed in the Senate. The first Jew to serve on the U.S Supreme Court almost did not make it.

Elite Americans were not the only ones who disliked and feared Jews. In the 1890s, a time of severe economic depression, the Populist party in the South and the Midwest claimed that greedy Jewish bankers and Wall Street tycoons had caused the country's economic misfortunes. Such accusations fanned the flames of anti-Semitism among the poorer classes of Americans, particularly in the South.

Anti-Semitism went beyond angry words against "the Jews." The story of Leo Frank dramatically shows how prejudice against the Jews became physical violence and how an innocent individual became the victim of a mob consumed by anti-Semitism. In the early 20th century Leo Frank had moved from New York to Atlanta, Georgia, where he owned a pencil factory. An active member of the Atlanta Jewish community, Frank was the president of the local B'nai B'rith lodge, an organization of Jewish men.

In 1913 the body of a 13-year-old girl named Mary Phagan was discovered in the basement of Frank's factory. She had been brutally attacked and disfigured. Although there was no evidence against Frank, the police arrested him for the crime. Still without evidence, the jury found him guilty and sentenced him to death. Governor John Slaton believed that Frank was innocent and that he had been found guilty because he was a Jew and a northerner. He reduced Leo Frank's sentence to life imprisonment and told some of his friends that he would soon pardon Frank because not a shred of evidence had linked Frank to the murder. But Tom Watson, a powerful speaker and writer who later became governor, stirred up the anti-Semitism of some Georgians, calling on

Many political conservatives opposed the appointment of Louis D. Brandeis to the U.S. Supreme Court in 1915. In this cartoon, corrupt conservatives lament the loss of a Supreme Court they had controlled and that Brandeis will reform.

them to avenge the girl's death, to show that Jews could not get away with murder. In the middle of the night, 25 men calling themselves the Knights of Mary Phagan kidnapped Leo Frank from his prison cell and hanged him from an oak tree near Mary Phagan's home. They made the name Leo Frank synonymous with American anti-Semitism and mob violence. (In 1985 the Georgia Board of Pardons posthumously pardoned Frank.)

American Jews—both newcomers and well-established people whose families had been in the United States for one or more generations—knew all too well that anti-Semitism existed. Some of them created organizations like the American Jewish Committee (1906) and the Anti-Defamation League (1913) to combat anti-Jewish rhetoric and behavior. They must have been terribly disappointed when the U.S. Congress passed the Johnson Act in 1924, ending a long American tradition of free and open immigration. The Jews who still lived in eastern Europe now had little chance of joining the millions already in the United States.

After 1924, American Jewish communities would increasingly be made up of people born in the United States, not immigrants. Life in Europe faded to a distant memory. Yet in the momentous decades to come, events in Europe would profoundly affect America's Jews. Despite the miles that separated them, Jews in the United States would still feel a link to their sisters and brothers around the world.

On April 16, 1915, Leo Frank was lynched in Georgia by an angry mob that believed he had murdered a young Christian girl, although there was no evidence to prove it. His fate stands as a powerful example of anti-Semitism in U.S. history.

Chapter 4

Becoming Americans: 1924–1945

The years between the Johnson Act of 1924 and the end of World War II in 1945 transformed American Jews. In fact, those years transformed all Americans. No one escaped completely from the ravages of the Great Depression during the 1930s or from World War II, which raged from 1939 to 1945 (the United States entered the war in 1941). But Jews experienced these cataclysmic events in a special way simply because they were Jewish.

Even if there had been no depression and no World War II, life would have changed for American Jews after the early 1920s. Once immigration stopped, the Jewish people in the United States became more and more *American* Jews, comfortable with a modern, urban way of life. With immigration from Europe halted, growth in the Jewish population of the United States would result from natural increase, births outnumbering deaths. In 1927 Jews made up about 3.6 percent of the American population. That percentage would stay the same for a time and then decrease. The proportion of Jews in the American population declined after the end of immigration.

The eastern European immigrants and their children who made up 80 percent of the Jews in the United States decided that in order to succeed they had to limit their family size. In the 19th century, Jews in Europe and the United States had typically had large families. They did

Hank Greenberg was a skillful baseball player who may have been American Jews' first popular hero.

not know how to limit the number of children, nor did they want to do so. Large families were desirable because children contributed to the family economically. Many children died young, so couples had large families to ensure that some would survive to support the parents in old age. That pattern changed in the United States during the 1920s and 1930s. By 1938 half of all Jewish families had no more than two children. They took advantage of advances in birth control technology to have small families, feeling that they could care for and educate two children at a level not possible for six or eight children.

At the height of immigration, Jewish families had faced many of the problems that troubled all poor people in the United States. Men who could not support their families felt ashamed; some deserted their wives and children. Jewish social workers, leaders of social settlement houses, and volunteers associated with organizations like the National Council of Jewish Women worried about divorce, crime, prostitution, juvenile delinquency, and other symptoms of disorganization that flared in the Jewish communities, particularly the larger ones. These problems did not go away. During the depression, which began in 1929 and did not really end until the United States entered World War II in 1941, Jewish families struggling with unemployment and underemployment faced these same difficulties. But by the time the massive immigration dwindled, American Jews were moving in a new direction.

For one thing, in the 1920s large numbers of Jews left the immigrant neighborhoods where they had built the institutions of their communities. For example, in 1916 353,000 Jews clustered in New York City's Lower East Side. By 1930 that number had fallen to 121,000. Jews headed for new sections of the Bronx and Brooklyn, two of New York's outer boroughs. Louis Wirth, a sociologist at the University of Chicago, traced the formation of the Jewish community in Chicago in his 1928 book *The Ghetto*. His chapter on the 1920s was titled "The Vanishing Ghetto." Chicago's Jews were moving out of the old immigrant neighborhood around Maxwell Street to the newer, more westerly Lawndale neighborhood. But Wirth noticed a trend. Even as some Jews were moving to this second area of settlement, many already had chosen a third. Wirth wrote,

"The area of third settlement, in Chicago as elsewhere, is located in the outlying residential sections of the city . . . a new frontier lying several miles from the area of second settlement."

These movements changed Jewish community life. In the first immigrant neighborhoods, families lived close to each other and to synagogues, schools, bakeries, butcher shops, settlement houses, and other community institutions where they met and carried on their social life. Family members often lived next door or within blocks of each other. People had convenient support networks.

Following the patterns of American city development, the farther out they went, the farther apart they lived and the less dense were their neighborhoods. Throughout the 1920s, 1930s, and 1940s Jews continued to live

More Jews lived in New York City than any other place in America, and the Lower East Side was the neighborhood where many settled upon arrival from Europe. On the streets there, people did business from pushcarts.

in predominantly Jewish neighborhoods, but those neighborhoods lacked the intense Jewish street life associated with immigrant times.

Another problem confronted Jews who moved to less dense areas. Jewish law prohibited traveling on the Sabbath in any kind of vehicle. Traditionally, though, Jews had lived within walking distance of the synagogue. What happened when they lived too far away to walk comfortably? At the same time that Jews were moving out of the neighborhoods of first settlement, levels of personal piety were declining and synagogue attendance was dropping. Now new housing arrangements forced Jews to compromise with traditional practice. Jews in Johnstown, Pennsylvania, adopted a common solution: They drove to synagogue on the Sabbath but parked their cars several blocks away. Out of respect for tradition, and perhaps because they felt a bit ashamed, they did not want to be seen violating Jewish law by parking right in front of a house of worship. Most Jews willingly relaxed the strict practice of tradition so that they could take advantage of new opportunities.

The Jews' geographic mobility was possible because so many families had left the working class to enter business and the professions. The daughters and sons of garment workers and pushcart peddlers became schoolteachers, social workers, bookkeepers, accountants, clerks, and salespeople. Those who chose to own businesses rarely took over their parents' little grocery stores but instead moved into more substantial enterprises. Many young Jewish people studied law and medicine. In 1920, for example, 14 percent of the students at 106 prestigious law schools were Jewish. At a time when very few women attended law school and became lawyers, the percentage of Jewish women in law schools was 14 percent of all women law students. This equaled that of Jews among male law students.

Although slowed somewhat by the depression, Jews continued to make economic progress. Yet they met discrimination from large corporations, hospitals, and other employers. Jews made up 26 percent of the population of New York City, but despite their high level of education held only 10 percent of all jobs in the professions and management.

The economic advancement of the first generation of American-born Jews came about because of the public schools they attended. Unlike many other groups of immigrants, the Jews did not create a separate school system to educate their children. Instead they sent their children to public schools in record numbers. As early as 1918, a time when most Americans did not attend high school, 53 percent of all New York high school students came from Jewish families. This strong emphasis on education may have reflected the Jewish tradition of respect for learning, especially religious learning. It also showed how strongly Jews wanted to leave the working class.

Education did not stop with high school. Young Jewish women and men viewed college as the route to a comfortable life. Nearly half of all college students in New York City were Jewish. Nationally, Jews made up less than 4 percent of the total population but more than 9 percent of all college students.

By the 1920s, the eastern European Jews who had come to the United States between 1880 and World War I had married and produced an American-born generation. These children understood Yiddish and had no doubt heard their parents' stories about how terrible life had been in the old country. Still, to them Europe was not even a memory. The immigrant generation had had to focus all their energy on the struggle to make a living. But their children had to figure out how to be both American and Jewish, how to live in two worlds, how to be comfortable with two

Jewish young people in New York and other big cities participated in the popular entertainments of the 20th century. These girls were off to Coney Island, the beachfront amusement park in Brooklyn. They also enjoyed movies, vaude-ville, shows, dance halls, and sports.

Speaking of Greenberg:
A Poem by Edgar A. Guest

Hank Greenberg became a baseball hero for all Americans, but Jews in particular took pleasure in his success on the diamond. When he refused to play ball on Yom Kippur in 1934, rather than antagonizing non-Jewish Detroiters who hoped for a victory, he won their admiration. Journalist and poet Edgar A. Guest composed this poem about the event that appeared in the Detroit Free Press *in 1934.*

The Irish didn't like it when they heard of Greenberg's fame
For they thought a good first baseman should possess an Irish name;
And the Murphys and Mulrooneys said they never dreamed they'd see
A Jewish boy from Bronxville out where Casey used to be.
In the early days of April not a Dugan tipped his hat
Or prayed to see a "double" when Hank Greenberg came to bat.
In July the Irish wondered where he'd ever learned to play.
"He makes me think of Casey!" Old Man Murphy dared to say;
And with fifty-seven doubles and a score of homers made
The respect they had for Greenberg was being openly displayed.
But upon the Jewish New Year when Hank Greenberg came to bat
And made two home runs off Pitcher Rhodes—
They cheered like mad for that.
Came Yom Kippur—holy feast day world wide over to the Jew—
And Hank Greenberg to his teaching and the old tradition true
Spent the day among his people and he didn't come to play.
Said Murphy to Mulrooney, "We shall lose the game today!
We shall miss him on the infield and shall miss him at the bat,
But he's true to his religion—and I honor him for that!"

cultures. The story of American Jews after 1924 is their story.

Hank Greenberg was one of many who had to balance Americanness and Jewishness. Born in 1911 in New York to immigrant parents, Hank developed a passion for baseball, which his parents considered a frivolous pastime. They wanted him to go to college, get an education, and become a professional. But Hank wanted to play ball. In 1933 he signed a contract with the Detroit Tigers, for whom he played for most of his career. A powerful hitter, this 6-foot-4-inch first baseman–outfielder might be considered the first real American Jewish superstar. Four times he led the American League in home runs. His 1937 RBI (runs batted in) record was only one run short of the league's best.

Gertrude Berg created the character of Molly Goldberg for radio and then for television. Molly was a warm, wise, Jewish housewife who dispensed chicken soup and good advice to her neighbors and children on the show and helped create a positive image of Jews in the mid-20th century.

In 1934 the Jewish holy day of Yom Kippur fell on September 19, a day the Tigers were scheduled to play a crucial game to keep their hopes for a pennant alive. That day Hank Greenberg put his identity as a Jew over loyalty to his team. Instead of heading for Tiger Stadium, he prayed with the congregation of Detroit's Shaarey Zedek ("gates of justice"). The Yankees beat Detroit 5-2. Even though Detroit lost, fans rallied behind him, respecting his religious stance.

Gertrude Berg's story shows how American Jews sometimes forged success by combining their Jewish backgrounds with American opportunities. Like Hank Greenberg, Berg started out in New York, where she was born Gertrude Edelstein in 1899. Her immigrant parents had succeeded in a small business and made a comfortable life for their children. Just as Greenberg loved baseball, Gertrude Edelstein had a passion for entertainment. She developed it at the Jewish resort her parents owned in the Catskill Mountains north of New York City. The hotel, like many popular Jewish vacation spots, featured theater, comedy arts, and other entertainment. In 1929, after studying drama part-time at Columbia University,

Berg came up with a great idea. She created a radio show called "The Rise of the Goldbergs." Drawing inspiration from her childhood, using parents and grandparents and family friends as models, Berg portrayed the life of an urban Jewish family with Molly Goldberg—played by Berg herself—at its center.

"The Rise of the Goldbergs" went on the air on an NBC radio station on November 20, 1929. At first it could be heard only in New York and only once a week. But it became so popular that by 1931 the network decided to let Americans all over the country hear it five nights a week. Americans of all religions and backgrounds came to know Berg's signature call to the woman next door, "Yoo hoo, Mrs. Bloom!" In one episode, "Molly's Fish," executives of a food company want Molly to work for them preparing her *gefilte* fish, a classic Jewish dish of chopped fish made for the Sabbath meal, for consumers around the country. But Molly cannot make her fish correctly in the company's big industrial kitchen—she needs the comfort and familiarity of her own apartment.

Another Jewish entertainer who became widely popular was Benny Goodman, born in Chicago in 1909 to immigrant parents. Goodman grew up in grinding poverty, living in the tough area around Maxwell Street. His father wanted to protect Benny and his brothers from the crime in the streets around them. When Benny was 10, his father enrolled him in a band at the Kehilath Jacob Synagogue. The band director gave young Goodman a clarinet. The boy fell in love with the instrument and went on to study music seriously at the Hull House Settlement.

Goodman put together his own band when he was only 18 and got work playing in jazz clubs around Chicago in the early 1920s. In 1926 he made his first recording. By the end of the decade Americans knew him as the "King of Swing," and he was on his way to becoming one of the most popular of all American musicians. Goodman broke all sorts of barriers. In 1936 he put together a band in which, for the first time, black and white musicians played together in public. In 1938, when he strode across the stage at New York's Carnegie Hall, he showed that popular American music belonged in the concert hall just as much as the dance hall. Greenberg, Berg, and Goodman became American heroes, but their fame and popularity moved American Jews in a special way. Their careers showed young Jewish men and women that the doors to success really had opened up to Jews. A person could be Jewish and still be a real American.

Popular culture was not the only area in which Jews succeeded between 1924 and 1945. In the struggle for social justice, Jewish women and men contributed to American life. Justine Wise Polier was certainly less widely known than Hank Greenberg, Benny Goodman, or Gertrude Berg, but her story represents an important development in the lives of American Jews.

Her father, Stephen Wise, was a prominent American rabbi. Her mother, Louise Waterman Wise, had achieved fame as a painter and also volunteered many hours in the Jewish community. Justine Wise Polier did not follow either of her parents' career paths. She could never have become a rabbi—it would be almost 50 years until Jewish women were allowed to become rabbis. And unlike her mother she was not content to be a volunteer, however worthy the cause. Justine did, however, share her parents' activism. As a passionate believer in the rights of workers, she joined the striking workers in the woolen mills in Passaic, New Jersey. One newspaper called her "Joan of Arc of the Mills." Her commitment to making the world a better place led her to Yale Law School. She graduated in 1927, one of five women in the class of 125.

When Justine Wise Polier was 32, Fiorello La Guardia, the mayor of New York, appointed her to a judgeship. She was the youngest municipal judge in the country and one of the few women to hold such a position. She wrote of her early years on the judge's bench, "I saw the vast chasms between our rhetoric of freedom, equality and charity, and what we were doing to, or not doing for, poor people, especially children."

Almost all American Jews were politically liberal. They wanted society to provide greater care to those in need, workers, the poor, children, and black people. Some Jews moved to the far left of American politics. The economic and social problems of the United States, even before the

From the time she was a young woman, Justine Wise, the daughter of Rabbi Stephen Wise, fought for issues of social justice and for the rights of children, women, and the poor. She participated in strikes in the textile industry in North Carolina in the late 1920s and then went on to law school and a judgeship.

The National Council of Jewish Women, founded in the 1890s, helped women educate themselves about Judaism and Jewish history, and gave them a way to serve their communities directly and to lobby for social welfare issues, particularly those concerning the rights of immigrants, women, and children. Here, members distribute books to cash-strapped public libraries during the depression.

depression, made the communist-led Soviet Union seem like a good model. Both immigrants and American-born Jews joined the Communist party and other left-wing organizations such as the International Workers' Order. They believed that these movements provided the best solution to all social problems.

But most American Jews directed their political loyalties to liberal movements within the mainstream parties. They admired and supported Democratic President Franklin D. Roosevelt and his New Deal, a set of programs that made the federal government an active agent in solving the problems of poverty and easing the distress of economic inequality. Roosevelt created his New Deal in response to the crises of the Great Depression, which began with the crash of the stock market in October 1929. The collapse of the American economy did not affect Jews quite as severely as other groups because so many Jews were self-employed. Tens of thousands of Jewish women and men, however, lost their jobs and Jewish institutions, synagogues, and charitable associations lost much of their financial backing because individuals could no longer afford to contribute to the community. Jewish parents faced with shrinking family budgets decided to save money by not giving their children Jewish education.

The depression played an important part in shaping Jews' ideas about themselves and the United States. In some ways it brought Jews closer to the American mainstream. Many Jews went to Washington, D.C., to work in New Deal programs. Jewish lawyers, prevented by prejudice from getting jobs in private law firms, had previously worked alone or in all-Jewish firms. Now they worked for the government. Jewish social workers also flocked to Washington to work in government agencies that dealt with social welfare. Jews could be found among Roosevelt's closest advisers. They included Harvard law professor and later Supreme Court Justice Felix Frankfurter, labor leader Sidney Hillman, and Henry Morgenthau, Jr., the secretary of the treasury. Some of Roosevelt's critics claimed that he had created not a New Deal but a "Jew Deal." They charged that Roosevelt was really a Jew; anti-Semitism increased their dislike of him and his policies.

The depression brought some negative lessons to American Jews, who realized that despite their progress they were not quite equal to everyone else. When times got bad, Jews were still a scapegoat upon whom Gentiles could vent their anger. The economic distress of the depression caused anti-Semitism to reach new highs.

Jews had been shocked in the 1920s when Henry Ford, the automobile pioneer, published false and insulting anti-Semitic material in his newspaper, the *Dearborn Independent*. One of the documents he published, called "The Protocols of the Elders of Zion," was a forgery that claimed to be a record of the secret meeting of a group of Jews who controlled the world's economy. It fueled the fires of anti-Semitism by encouraging people to believe that a secret conspiracy of Jews was out to ruin everyone else.

Jews also watched with alarm in the 1920s as the Ku Klux Klan spread beyond its traditional base to become a powerful voice against them. The Klan of the 1870s had been limited to the South. Its mission

Henry Morgenthau, Jr., was a friend, neighbor, and personal confidant of President Franklin Roosevelt, who appointed him secretary of the Treasury. While Morgenthau served in that capacity, Europe's Jews underwent the crisis of Nazism and World War II. Morgenthau tried quietly to get the U.S. government to help them, but his efforts amounted to too little.

was to terrorize newly freed black people, keeping them from voting and exercising their other constitutional rights. But the newly revived Klan of the 1920s appealed to some people by arguing that Jews and Catholics had taken over the country. Jews, the Klan claimed, were Communists bent on destroying American civilization. The Klan's claims were absurd and illogical—despite the fact that Communists were opposed to private banking and finance, the Klan also claimed that Jews owned the banks and corporations that stole the livelihoods of "real" Americans, who were Christian and white.

Even before the depression, anti-Semitism had reminded American Jews of prejudice and pogroms. For example, two days before Yom Kippur in 1928, a small child in upstate New York wandered off into the woods. A local mayor, clergymen, and state troopers thought that Jews might be responsible. They asked the local rabbi if Jews sacrificed Christian children on this particular holiday.

The 1920s also saw the formalization of discrimination against Jews at colleges and universities, which used quotas to keep Jewish students out. Many American neighborhoods also kept Jews out by means of restrictive covenants. These statements attached to deeds of land ownership declared that the owner could never sell to Jews or blacks. Such practices and trends worsened during the 1930s, when anti-Jewish rhetoric reached much larger audiences.

In 1936 Father Charles Coughlin, a Catholic priest from Detroit, preached over the radio to an audience of 20 to 30 million listeners. He told them that Jews had caused their economic suffering. Coughlin was not alone. More than 100 anti-Semitic organizations were founded in the 1930s, mostly in response to the depression. Sometimes anti-Semitism involved more than words. From 1939 through 1942, gangs inspired by

Coughlin desecrated synagogues, attacked Jewish children and adults on the streets of New York, and scrawled obscene messages on the walls of Jewish-owned businesses.

The first public opinion polls appeared in the 1930s, and some of them show how uncomfortable the United States could be for Jews. In 1938, for example, about 50 percent of all Americans admitted that they had a negative view of Jews, and about 60 percent agreed with the statement that Jews were by and large greedy, dishonest, and aggressive. In 1942, pollsters asked high school students who they would not want as a roommate when they went off to college. Of the respondents, 3 percent said "Irish" or "don't know," but 45 percent named Jews. Only blacks received a higher—or lower—score: 78 percent. Only 5 percent of the students polled shrugged off the question and said that they did not care.

How to respond to growing anti-Semitism? American Jews were divided. Many of those who were comfortable and well established thought it best to ignore anti-Semitism, hoping that it would disappear when the depression ended. Those who felt that something should be done favored quiet, behind-the-scenes action and did not want the subject discussed in the newspapers.

On a personal level, many Jews changed their names so that they would not stand out as Jewish. From the 1930s through 1945 in Los Angeles, Jews were more likely than any other people to go to court to change their names. One Hollywood writer, Abraham Polansky, told an interviewer: "When I arrived at Paramount [movie studio] as a contract writer, another Jewish writer told me to change my name. He told me it sounded Jewish and that movies were seen all over America. I didn't change my name . . . but many actors did. Americans wanted to see Americans." So actor Julius Garfinkle became Jules Garfield. Then his studio, Warner Brothers, made him change his name again, to John Garfield. Emanuel Goldberg became Edward G. Robinson. Melvyn Hesselberg became Melvyn Douglas. Marion Levy became Paulette Goddard. Betty Persky became Lauren Bacall. All were among the leading stars of their time.

Jews who felt uncomfortable about being identified as Jews distanced themselves from community institutions. And they did not like Jews to make themselves visible in politics or popular culture, fearing that this would cause Gentiles to blame all Jews for the deeds or the prominence of some.

Other Jews, however, worried that young Jews would grow up ashamed to be Jewish, that they would want to escape from the burdens that they faced. They might leave the Jewish community and tradition behind—at worst they might convert to Christianity. Perhaps they would decide that being Jewish was just not worth the pain.

Psychologist Kurt Lewin came to the United States from Germany in the early 1930s. He believed that anti-Semitism caused irreparable psychological damage to Jewish children. Lewin recognized the reality of anti-Semitism, but he thought that ignoring it was worse than fighting it. He advised Jewish parents to give their children positive feelings about Jewishness and a strong sense of belonging to the community and the tradition. This, he believed, would prepare them for their unavoidable encounters with anti-Semitism.

Lewin was not alone in trying to find ways to strengthen the Jewish bond at a time when young Jews wanted very much to enter the American mainstream. In synagogues, in the field of Jewish education, in the Zionist movement, and in other Jewish community institutions, Jews tried to create new ties and strengthen old ones to ensure the survival of Judaism in the United States. Jewish organizations created dozens of summer camps, primarily for youngsters but also for adults. The camps' founders hoped to create an all-Jewish environment where people could have fun and be Jewish at the same time, with experiences that included sports, swimming, crafts, the Hebrew or Yiddish language, and Jewish music.

But summer camp lasted only for a few weeks. How could Jews revitalize Jewish life in the United States all year round? In 1934 Mordecai Kaplan tried to answer that question in a book titled *Judaism as a Civilization*. Kaplan had experienced a completely traditional eastern European Jewish upbringing. Born in Lithuania, he had attended the Etz

Chaim Yeshiva as a boy in New York and then graduated from the more American-oriented Jewish Theological Seminary (JTS). Through the 1910s and 1920s Kaplan moved farther and farther away from his traditional background. He believed that the feelings that gave life to Judaism in eastern Europe could not really appeal to young, educated American Jews. He was convinced that the prayer books and other texts that had remained unchanged for generations had to change to keep the loyalty of the American-born generation—they had to speak the language and express the feelings of the American culture in which they lived.

In *Judaism as a Civilization* Kaplan argued that American Jews really lived in two worlds, one American and one Jewish. The two worlds had to fit together, which meant that Judaism had to adapt to American conditions. But unlike the members of the Reform movement, Kaplan believed strongly in the idea of Jewish peoplehood. He thought that Reform temples worried too much about decorum and order and lacked the warmth and friendliness that most human beings craved.

Kaplan also differed with Reform Jews on the question of how and when to change rituals and texts inherited from the past. He did not want to completely discard traditional practices unless they strongly clashed with American values. When conflicts arose between tradition and new circumstances, groups of Jews—both rabbis and laypeople—should democratically discuss the issues and decide what to keep and what to change. For example, Kaplan thought that Jews should use the democratic process to decide whether or not they approved of driving a car on the

Mordecai Kaplan (left) believed that Judaism needed to be reconstructed in America in order to make sense in the 20th century. He created the Reconstructionist movement as an alternative to Conservatism, Orthodoxy, and Reform Judaism.

Sabbath. He often said that Jewish law and tradition should have "a vote but not a veto." In other words, it should be part of the decision-making process but should not dictate everything about what American Jews could and could not do.

In 1941, together with followers who called themselves Reconstructionists, Kaplan published a new *haggadah* (the prayer book used at the *seder,* the Passover meal). In 1945 they issued a new prayer book. *The New Haggadah* was popular with many American Jews, even those who may have not agreed with all of Kaplan's philosophy and had never heard the term "Reconstructionist." But the more traditional Jews, including many of Kaplan's colleagues at JTS, condemned *The New Haggadah.* They found Kaplan, his supporters, and their ideas unacceptable. Among other objections, they did not approve of the way Kaplan had removed references to the Jews as the "chosen people," and they felt that by including nontraditional materials such as the African-American spiritual "Go Down Moses" he had produced a book that was not truly Jewish.

In 1945 a group of Orthodox rabbis held a book-burning ceremony in New York. They burned copies of Kaplan's prayer book and placed a *herem* (a ban of excommunication that excluded someone from the Jewish faith and community) on Kaplan. Their actions, however, did little to halt the spread of Kaplan's ideas. Very few Jews actually joined Kaplan's Reconstructionist movement, but rabbis and laypeople from both Conservative and Reform Judaism liked his ideas and absorbed them into their forms of Judaism.

While some American Jews were trying to remake Judaism and its institutions, others saw that Jews outside the United States were facing some of the greatest crises of their long history. A number of American Jews tried valiantly to try to help the Jewish people worldwide.

Abba Hillel Silver was one of them. Like Mordecai Kaplan, he had been born in Lithuania. He arrived in New York in 1902 at the age of nine. He quickly learned English, attended American schools, and seemed pretty much like any other American Jewish youngster. Even as a teenager, however, he was recognized by his peers as an outstanding speaker and a devoted follower of Zionism, the political and cultural movement dedicated to creating a Jewish homeland in Palestine.

Silver and some of his friends organized the Dr. Herzl Zion Club, named for Theodor Herzl, the founder of the Zionist movement. The club met at the Educational Alliance. One day some members of the board came to inspect the clubs and classes meeting at the settlement house. They were very nervous about Zionism, fearing that Gentile Americans would consider Jews disloyal to the United States if they supported the cause of a Jewish Palestine. When these inspectors discovered the meeting of the Dr. Herzl Zion Club they expressed their unhappiness at the club's name, its purpose, and the fact that the club conducted its business in Hebrew, not English. Silver replied that the young people had the right to choose any name that they wanted for their club, that they did not care what others would think of them because of their ideas, and that the language that had been good enough for King David to use when writing the Psalms and the prophet Isaiah when preaching about universal peace was surely good enough for the Educational Alliance.

Silver graduated from the Hebrew Union College (HUC) in 1915. This was unusual for someone from eastern European Orthodox roots who believed strongly in the creation of a Jewish homeland because the HUC, the rabbinical seminary for Reform rabbis, tended to attract young men of German background and few Zionists. Silver briefly served as a rabbi in Wheeling, West Virginia. In 1917 he accepted one of the most prestigious pulpits in the United States, Cleveland's Congregation Tifereth Israel, known as The Temple. Silver gave Sunday morning lectures to thousands of Clevelanders, Gentiles as well as Jews. He also participated in numerous progressive causes, defending the rights of immigrants, freedom of speech, and the right of workers to organize in labor unions.

Most members of The Temple's Reform congregation were prosperous and felt perfectly comfortable with the formalism of The Temple, the use of English in services, and the fact that previous rabbis had discarded many rituals. But Silver convinced them that Hebrew was the language of the Jewish people and should be prominently featured in service and in

Rabbi Abba Hillel Silver played a crucial role in American Zionism, particularly in the dark years of World War II. He believed that the only solution to the crisis of Europe's Jews, now referred to as the Holocaust, would be found in the immediate creation of an independent Jewish state in Palestine, the Jews' ancestral homeland.

the religious school. He also made enemies among the congregation by trying to restore elements of Jewish practice that earlier rabbis had eliminated. For example, in the last decades of the 19th century many Reform congregations had eliminated the *bar mitzvah,* a ritual that marked a boy's entry into manhood within the Jewish community. Reform groups had replaced the *bar mitzvah* with confirmation for both boys and girls, modeling this ceremony on Protestant rituals. Silver decided to keep confirmation but return to the *bar mitzvah* as well.

Silver's most important public activities, however, were related to Zionism and world Jewry. American Jews were shocked when Adolf Hitler came to power in Germany in 1933. For 10 years they had read about the Nazi party, but like most Americans—and probably most liberal Germans—they had not believed that such an antidemocratic and anti-Semitic party could ever win control of the country. They had not thought that Hitler, who had expressed his dream of killing all Jews as early as 1925 in his book *Mein Kampf* (My Struggle), could ever win over the German people.

They were wrong. In January 1933 Hitler became the chancellor of Germany and set in motion a series of actions, edicts, and decisions that would bring about the Holocaust, the systematic murder of 6 million European Jews.

From then until the end of World War II in 1945, American Jews could not agree among themselves what course of action they should, or could, take to defeat Nazism and rescue the Jewish people. They tried to change U.S. immigration policy, a system setting a limit on the number of immigrants by country of origin, figuring that temporary changes in the quota system could rescue some European Jews. They failed in this effort. About 150,000 refugees did manage to enter the United States in the 1930s and 1940s, but American public opinion, the U.S. Congress, and even Franklin Roosevelt did not want to change immigration laws and policies.

Abba Hillel Silver played an important role in another early plan, which called for an American boycott of German goods. Silver believed that if all Americans, led and inspired by Jews, refused to buy German products, the German economy would collapse and the German people would rise up and remove Hitler from power. He could not, however, win broad support for this proposal.

During the 1930s the Nazis became more secure in their power and began to act upon their threatened campaign against the Jews of Germany. They also extended their control over Austria and Czechoslovakia, which had substantial Jewish populations. Seeing these events unfold in Europe, Silver and other Zionists came to a conclusion that disturbed many other leaders of the American Jewish community. They decided that the only way to solve the critical problem of Europe's Jews lay in an independent, sovereign Jewish state in Palestine. It did no good to try to move small groups of Jews to other havens. Only a homeland over which Jewish people had sovereignty could solve the looming crisis.

Jews had been migrating to Palestine for more than 50 years in order to reestablish a Jewish presence there. However, since the end of World War I in 1918 Great Britain had had control over Palestine. In 1936, just as life became significantly more frightening for the Jews of Europe, Great

Britain drastically limited the number of Jews who could enter Palestine. The Jews of Europe were trapped. Some Jews of the United States considered it their responsibility to help.

Silver opposed what he considered "refugeeism"—the efforts of Jewish communities in the United States to help refugees fleeing Hitler. He did not want to withhold assistance from the desperate Jews who did make it to the United States, and he certainly approved of the aid that most large American Jewish communities offered to the refugees, helping them find housing and jobs. But millions more had no place to go, and Silver did not want American Jews to forget them.

As a leading officer of two important Jewish fund-raising organizations, the United Palestine Appeal and the United Jewish Appeal (UJA), Silver brought American Jewish public opinion to his side. After war broke out in Europe in 1939, exposing millions of Jews in Poland and the rest of eastern Europe to the savagery of the German military, Silver used brilliant oratory to convince American Jews to press the U.S. government to support the idea of a Jewish state. "Freedom," thundered Abba Hillel Silver, "must be taken," and freedom for Jews meant statehood. The vision of a homeland for the Jews, Silver declared, "is the cry of desperation of a people driven to the wall, fighting for its very life. Zionism is not self-pity. . . . It is the pressing urgency of instant and current suffering . . . . Enough! There must be an end to all this! A sure and certain end!"

By May 1942 American Jews knew some of what the Nazis were doing in Europe—enough to understand the imminent doom of European Jewry. The only people who could do anything at all to prevent it were the Jews of the United States. At a meeting in New York's Biltmore Hotel Silver brought even the timid to their feet when he insisted that the American Zionist movement commit itself once and for all to demanding an independent Jewish homeland in Palestine.

During the war years Zionism captured the imagination and loyalty of most American Jews. What had been a marginal and small movement, opposed by some Jews, became a rallying cry. In the 1930s the Reform movement, which had declared itself opposed to Zionism at the end of

The Zionist Paragraphs in the Columbus Platform

The crisis of German Jewry after the rise of Hitler and the Nazis to power in 1933 had a powerful effect on American Jews and their institutions. The Reform movement had not supported the idea of a Jewish homeland in Palestine. But by the 1930s the tide had turned and the rabbis and laypeople in Reform congregations had come to believe that millions of Jews were not safe and only a land of their own could protect them. In the Columbus Platform, drafted at a meeting in 1937, the rabbis affirmed thier support for a Jewish homeland in Palestine.

Judaism is the soul of which Israel [the Jewish people] is the body. Living in all parts of the world, Israel has been held together by the ties of a common history, and above all, by the heritage of faith. Though we recognize in the group-loyalty of Jews who have become estranged from our religious tradition, a bond which still unites them with us, we maintain that it is by its religion and for its religion that the Jewish people has lived. The non-Jew who accepts our faith is welcomed as a full member of the Jewish community.

In all lands where our people live, they assume and seek to share loyally the full duties and responsibilities of citizenship and to create seats of Jewish knowledge and religion. In the rehabilitation of Palestine, the land hallowed by our memories and hopes, we behold the promise of renewed life for many of our brethren. We affirm the obligation of all Jewry to aid in its upbuilding as a Jewish homeland by endeavoring to make it not only a haven of refuge for the oppressed but also a center of Jewish culture and spiritual life.

Throughout the ages it has been Israel's mission to witness to the Divine in the face of every form of paganism and materialism. We regard it as our historic task to cooperate with all men in the establishment of the kingdom of God, of universal brotherhood, justice, truth and peace on earth. This is our Messianic goal.

Jewish soldiers attend religious services at Buckingham Army Air Field in Fort Myers, Florida, in 1944. Jewish soldiers fought in the war as not only as a patriotic act but as part of their Jewish obligation to help rid the world of Hitler and Nazism.

the 19th century, threw its support behind Zionism. In 1937 the Central Conference of American Rabbis declared itself in favor of the Zionist cause. Even the American Jewish Committee, which had long thought that American Jews should not publicly embrace the idea of a Jewish state, joined the majority and stopped opposing Zionism.

By 1948, three years after the war ended and on the eve of the birth of the Jewish state of Israel, more than a million American Jews belonged to some kind of Zionist organization. Another million belonged to organizations like the B'nai B'rith, which although not officially Zionist agreed with the basic principles of Zionism.

We cannot know if American Jews supported Zionism solely because of the tragedy in Europe. Perhaps they liked the idea of a Jewish state because they were stung by the anti-Semitic rhetoric they heard in the

United States. Anti-Semitism, however, declined after the war. It reached an all-time high in 1944, as measured by opinion polls, and then dropped dramatically in 1945. Never again would it rise to the level of the Great Depression and the early 1940s.

World War II had transformed the status of Jews in the United States. They participated enthusiastically in the war effort because of their special stake in the war—Hitler's destruction of the European Jews—and their growing sense of themselves as Americans.

The Bureau of War Records of the Jewish Welfare Board collected and published information about Jewish participation in the U.S. military during the war. Jewish soldiers made up 8 percent of the military, double their percentage of the population as a whole. A total of 40,000 Jewish soldiers gave their lives; 36,000 received medals for distinguished service. Hank Greenberg hung up his Tigers uniform and volunteered to wear an Army one. Benny Goodman picked up his clarinet and played for the troops.

Most of the 150,000 German, Austrian, and Czechoslovakian Jews who came to the United States during the war were of humble origins. But a few, often called the refugee intellectuals, were scientists, architects, academics, writers, musicians, artists, psychotherapists, and philosophers. The best known of these was Albert Einstein, a physicist and winner of the Nobel Prize. He fled Germany to settle in Princeton, New Jersey, and became a leading figure in American science.

Like most Americans, Jews shared the prosperity that accompanied the boom economy of wartime production and rejoiced at the war's end in August 1945. But they were not the same as other Americans. As Jewish individuals, families, and communities jumped into the postwar move to suburbia, entering another chapter in their history, they carried with them the harrowing events of the Holocaust and the intense anti-Semitism they had experienced "even in America." These would haunt American Jews for decades to come.

Chapter 5

On the Move: 1945–1967

Abraham Levitt and his sons William and Alfred had been in the business of building houses since 1929. Even during the desperation of the depression and the shortages of the war years, Levitt and Sons managed to build massive tracts of new housing at relatively low cost in a kind of assembly-line style.

For the Levitt family—and for tens of thousands of young American families eager to own their own houses—the good times began when World War II ended. In 1946 Levitt and Sons began plans for the biggest private housing project in American history. Set on an undeveloped stretch of land near the town of Hempstead on New York's Long Island, the project was called Island of Trees. Eventually, however, it took the name of Levittown.

The rush of Americans to the suburbs did not begin with Levittown, but the postwar era took on much of its character from the movement of people from cities to suburbs. The eager rush of Jews to the suburbs outside New York, Philadelphia, Chicago, Cleveland, and other cities shaped the way they lived, as Jews and as Americans.

Jews did not move just to the suburban fringes of the cities where they had grown up. They moved all over. Young Jews, generally more educated than the average American, eagerly looked for professional opportunities wherever they could find them. Studies of many communities in the 1960s

Young mothers stroll with their babies at the shopping center in Levittown, New York. Young Jewish couples, like their non-Jewish counterparts, streamed to the suburbs in the 1950s in search of better housing and living conditions than those in the urban neighborhoods of their parents.

Jewish institutions, like the Jewish Community Center (JCC) of Washington, D.C., had to respond to the suburban exodus. In some cases the institution left the city as well. The JCC moved from its stately building on 16th Street, just a few blocks from the White House, to build this sprawling structure in Rockville, Maryland, in the late 1960s.

found that up to a third of the Jews had come there from elsewhere.

California most dramatically shows how mobile Jews had become. In 1945 the Jewish population of Los Angeles numbered 150,000. By 1968 that number had grown to 510,000. Florida also experienced tremendous growth after World War II, and Jews contributed to that growth, settling in the suburbs.

Jews may have become suburbanites faster and in larger proportion than most Americans. By 1958 85 percent of the Jews in the Cleveland area lived beyond the city limits. In the 1960s the push to the suburbs took place in every Jewish community in the United States. For other groups suburbanization occurred more slowly—according to the U.S. Census it was not until 1970 that more Americans lived in suburbs than in cities.

When Jews moved to the suburbs they took many of their institutions with them. Synagogues, schools, and old-age homes migrated from city centers to new suburban neighborhoods. In 1969, for example, the Jewish Community Center (JCC) in Washington, D.C., moved from the quarters it had occupied since the 1920s in a stately building a mile or so from the White House to Rockville, a relatively distant suburb in Montgomery County, Maryland. But the JCC did not lead the Jewish population to the suburbs. It followed. Jewish families had already moved to the suburbs and wanted the JCC to be near their homes.

Throughout their history in the United States most Jews had been city-dwellers, a fact that had set them apart from the rest of the nation.

When most Americans lived on farms and small towns and made a living farming, Jews lived in the largest cities and earned their incomes from commerce and industry.

Still, American Jews had also been people on the move, migrating rapidly from the area of first settlement to better housing whenever they could. Their earlier moves, however, had been from one heavily Jewish neighborhood to another.

The urban neighborhoods of the immigrants and the first American-born generation were distinctive Jewish communities. They had not only synagogues and Hebrew schools but also kosher meat markets, bakeries, and restaurants, as well as Jewish theaters and bookstores in the larger cities. These institutions made it possible to "be" Jewish just by living in a neighborhood.

Even if a Jewish family did not belong to a synagogue, buy kosher food, or send their children to a school for Jewish education, life in a predominantly Jewish neighborhood shaped their identity. They were surrounded by Jews, and they did not have to think much about why they were Jewish or what that meant.

Some Jews became conscious of their Jewishness only when they met with hostility. When children who lived in heavily Jewish neighborhoods ventured out of those areas, people sometimes called them "dirty Jew," "Christ killer," or "kike." These ugly words made them feel Jewish, but not in a positive way.

Now the Jews were becoming suburbanites. Suburban life in Levittown and elsewhere changed the fabric of Jewish existence. People in the suburbs lived far apart from each other, not crowded together in apartments and rowhouses. The informal Jewish life of the big cities, much of which took place on the sidewalks, did not appear in the suburbs, where there were often no sidewalks and everyone got around by car.

Suburban Jews had many more non-Jewish neighbors than they had had in the cities. In areas where Jews accounted for no more than 20 or 25 percent of the population, shops and stores that specialized in Jewish goods had little chance of succeeding.

In suburban public schools and on playgrounds, Jewish and non-Jewish children mixed. Jewish children developed close relations with non-Jewish children in ways that would have been impossible for their parents and grandparents. The hostility that Jewish children had faced in the previous generation had pretty much faded. In the suburbs, Jewish children played the same games and joined the same clubs as Gentile children.

Popular culture continued to be a leveling force. The move to suburbia coincided with the first decade of television. Jewish children watched and enjoyed the same shows as their Protestant and Catholic neighbors. Many of those shows depicted a happy suburban life in which no one was Jewish. The television industry was similar to the movie industry—although many producers, directors, and writers were Jewish, they presented American life in a very bland way with little ethnic or religious character. When Gertrude Berg's radio show about the Goldberg family moved to television, a menorah on the mantelpiece was the only clue that the show was about a Jewish family. In the show, the Goldbergs moved to the fictional suburb of Haverstraw. Like much of American popular culture during the postwar period, "The Goldbergs" celebrated the suburban way of life.

What did it mean for Jewish children to grow up in these suburbs? How could parents give their children some sense of Jewish identity in this new environment? Jewishness had always been based on the idea of Jews as a distinctive people, but suburban life emphasized the importance of "fitting in."

The young couples with small children who flocked to the suburbs faced these quandaries right away. The parents may have had a deep sense of being Jewish because they had grown up with immigrant grandparents and come of age in Jewish neighborhoods. Their suburban children would need something else, something more formal to guide them in learning to be Jewish.

Jewish parents in the suburbs of the 1950s and 1960s turned to the synagogues. In the years after World War II Americans as a whole were turning—or returning—to formal religious membership and

The Boy Scouts of America allowed synagogues to form Jewish troops. These troops could award a special badge in Jewish learning, called the Ner Tamid (eternal light) award.

participation. In the brand-new housing developments such as Levittown, families flocked to houses of worship of every denomination. Jews were no different.

However, Jews did not build and join synagogues just because the Catholics or Methodists or Baptists around them were building and joining churches. Instead the Jews, like the Christians, found religion a comfortable way to organize their social life. They were all living in new communities, no longer in ethnic clusters surrounded by family. Churches and synagogues provided a link to something familiar. The American people had undergone the poverty of the Great Depression and the horrors of a world war. Moving to the suburbs was a lot like starting over afresh, and religion seemed like a meaningful part of this new life.

In the suburbs Jews built synagogues as they never had before. Between 1947 and 1959 they created 99 new congregations in the suburbs of New York City alone. Between 1945 and 1952 Jews spent somewhere between $50 and $60 million on new synagogue buildings—and in the next decade they doubled the amount of money spent for synagogue construction. Add to that the salaries for rabbis, cantors, and religious school

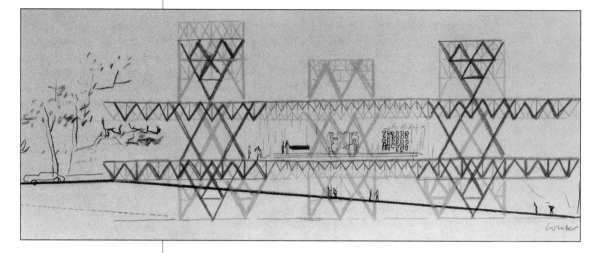

Philadelphia's Congregation Mikveh Israel commissioned the architect Louis Kahn to design a new structure in the 1960s. The congregation was Orthodox, but the architect used some of the most modern ideas of building, including some borrowed from Buckminster Fuller, a daring architectural visionary, for this preliminary sketch. Jews wanted new buildings that fit their status as full participants in modern American life.

directors and it becomes clear that American Jews made a substantial investment in Jewish life.

Congregations put up imposing buildings in the modern style. The synagogues were surrounded by parking lots—everyone drove to them. The typical synagogue was situated in a lovely, green, parklike setting with ample playground equipment to accommodate families with young children. Inside the building, the classrooms for the religious school, meeting rooms for the many clubs that met in the synagogue, and a large social hall with a well-equipped kitchen took up more space than the sanctuary where religious services were held. The sanctuary, though, usually had stained-glass windows, plush theater-style seats, and thick carpeting.

Suburban synagogues got full-time use. On weekday mornings a nursery school usually occupied the classrooms. The sisterhood and other clubs for women scheduled meetings during the daytime hours, because in those years most women did not work outside the home, although they volunteered a great deal of time to their synagogues. In the afternoon, once public school ended for the day, children flocked to the synagogue for religious school, filling up the classrooms again. Other rooms held evening meetings for boys and their *bar mitzvah* tutors, who helped them learn the material they would chant or read on the day of the ritual. Later, when congregations began holding *bat mitzvah* ceremonies for girls, the girls and their tutors also met at the synagogue. So did the men's club, teen groups, Boy Scout troops, and various committees of the congregation. Rehearsals for theatrical performances took place on the stage in the social hall, and dances for teens or adults were held there on weekends.

The activity with the lowest turnout and the least scheduled time was religious worship. Jews in the suburbs attended synagogue significantly less often than their Christian neighbors attended church. A 1958 survey found that 18 percent of Jews attended weekly services, as opposed to 76 percent of Catholics and 40 percent of Protestants. Few synagogues could pull together a *minyan,* the group of 10 men required for daily prayers. Saturday services rarely drew a big crowd unless there was a *bar mitzvah* or some other special event to celebrate.

Jews had not experienced a revival of religion in the sense of feeling heightened spiritual yearnings. Although rates of synagogue membership grew, the actual observance of religious ritual declined. Instead, suburban Jews had turned to the synagogue for the social and personal connections that in the cities had taken place in more informal places such as stores and sidewalks. The synagogue had replaced the Jewish neighborhood.

Nevertheless, the synagogue *was* a religious institution. Synagogues were either Reform, Orthodox, or Conservative. Their rabbis and cantors (singers who helped lead the worship service) had been trained in denominational seminaries. Each congregation belonged to one of the national, denominational associations: the Union of American Hebrew Congregations for the Reform, the United Synagogue of America for the Conservatives, or the Union of Orthodox Jewish Congregations for the Orthodox.

Despite denominational differences, all rabbis considered the synagogue's religious work to be its most important function. Rabbis from all three movements tried to get people to think of the synagogue as more than a place to meet friends or teach children some of the basics of Judaism. They wanted members to develop a connection to traditional rituals and worship services. They wanted to emphasize the spiritual side of Judaism, as opposed to the social side. In all three denominations a large gap separated the rabbis from the ordinary members. Rabbis and members had different ideas about the synagogue's purpose.

In the 1950s Conservative Judaism, the youngest branch of American Judaism, became its largest denomination. For 40 years the vast majority of American Jews who belonged to a congregation had been Orthodox. But starting in the 1940s Conservative Judaism grew faster than either Orthodox or Reform, and in the 1950s some Orthodox congregations switched to Conservative.

Conservative congregations offered religious services that seemed to fit suburban life. Unlike Orthodox congregations, Conservative men and women sat together, ending a traditional separation by gender that seemed to conflict with the growing importance of women as members and activists in the synagogue, in the Jewish community's volunteer work, and in American society.

Conservative congregations used a new prayer book, the *Sabbath and Festival Prayer Book* (1946). Its editor, Rabbi Morris Silverman, left most of the Hebrew text intact but presented the English translations in ways that did not seem out of place in the United States. For example, Jewish tradition emphasized the idea that the Jews had been "chosen" by God, but this seemed strange to American Jews, who believed in the American vision of equality. Silverman's prayer book presented the concept of the "chosen people" loosely rather than literally.

Some English was used in Conservative services, but most of the service continued to be in Hebrew. This is another way in which the Silverman prayer book tried to be both traditional and modern. The Orthodox used only Hebrew, while the Reform used mostly English.

The Conservative rabbi often wore an elegant robe like that of a Protestant minister, but over it he draped a *tallith*, the traditional fringed prayer shawl. He spoke well and put a great deal of effort into an uplifting sermon that often linked the portion of the Torah read that week to some issue of current affairs and common interest.

Some Conservative congregations had organs and choirs. Others did not, believing these elements too close to Reform Judaism or to Christianity, but even they relied on a cantor to lead the congregation in

communal singing. His dominating voice could cover up the fact that many of the congregants did not really know the prayers.

Conservative Judaism stressed the importance of Jewish law and organized a Committee on Jewish Law and Standards to decide how Jewish law applied to particular circumstances. Two of the committee's path-breaking decisions of the 1950s reveal much about American Jews in those years. In 1950 the committee ruled that Conservative Jews could drive in their cars to synagogue. In 1954 it decided that women could be called to the Torah to recite the blessings over the sacred scroll. In these and other rulings, Conservative Judaism willingly recognized reality—the fact that Jews lived in suburbs and could not walk to synagogue and the fact that women were gaining equality with men in many areas of society.

The 1954 decision to include women in the *minyan* grew out of the fact that increasing numbers of Jewish girls in Conservative congregations were having a *bat mitzvah*, ceremonies to mark their 13th birthdays,

Conservative congregations, like this Boston synagogue, differed from Orthodox ones by allowing men and women to sit together. Like all Jewish congregations, however, they expected aesthetically pleasing surroundings.

In the 1960s many girls began to celebrate their *bat mitzvah*, a ceremony to mark their 13th birthday and their approaching adulthood in the Jewish community. During the service, girls were allowed to read from the Torah scroll, traditionally an activity closed to them.

just as boys had traditionally had bar mitzvahs. The first bat mitzvah had taken place in 1922, when Mordecai Kaplan called his daughter Judith to the Torah, and the ceremony gained in popularity.

Suburban Jews of the postwar period had learned about Judaism from their Orthodox grandparents. To them, Conservative Judaism had familiar elements but still fit in with the life that Jews led as modern Americans. Reform Judaism was simply too big a leap. For example, in a Conservative synagogue men followed tradition by covering their heads with a special cap called a *yarmulke* (or *kippah*) and wearing a *tallith*, but in Reform congregations most men prayed with bare heads and no prayer shawl. Most members of the Conservative congregations did not follow tradition closely in their own lives, but praying without a head covering or prayer shawl just seemed wrong to them. On the other hand, Orthodoxy was not American enough for the educated, professional women and men who made up the Jewish suburban population. It created too large a gap between their everyday lives and their Jewish ones. Conservatism, with its strong emphasis on both tradition and the unity of the Jewish people, felt like the perfect blend of Jewishness and Americanness.

Some Jewish institutions did not make it to the suburbs. One by one, as the elderly remnants of the immigrant generation died, the old-fashioned *shtiebelach,* or little houses of prayer, folded. Young Jews did not reproduce them in the suburbs. Secular Jewish institutions outside the synagogue also had little success in the suburbs. Many of those secular institutions had been based on socialism and reflected the large number of Jews in the working class and the labor movement. By the 1940s, however, few Jews were laborers. Some of the secular institutions survived in the larger cities, especially New York, but their membership shrank as time went on. The Jews who owned businesses or worked as professionals and managers did not find the Arbeiter Ring (Workmen's Circle) or the Sholom Aleichem schools and summer camps particularly attractive.

Radical Jewish organizations also faded. The political climate of the United States had become inhospitable to them. The 1950s were not a comfortable time for a minority group such as the Jews to be allied with left-wing causes. In the years after World War II the United States engaged in a cold war against the Soviet Union and its political system, communism. Led by Senator Joseph McCarthy, some Americans made anticommunism a crusade and worked to identify and expose people they believed were or had been Communists. They wanted people with Communist sympathies banned from teaching in public schools, working in the government, and participating in film or television production. Public hostility toward Jews who had been associated with left-wing organizations got a boost in 1953 when a Jewish couple named Julius and Ethel Rosenberg were executed in New York's Sing Sing prison. They had been convicted of stealing highly secret documents from the United States and giving them to the Soviet Union. Other Jews lost their jobs in the motion picture industry.

Even Zionism failed to become a powerful force among suburban Jews. Ordinary Jewish women and men of the postwar years had very positive feelings about Israel, rejoiced when Israel declared its independence on May 14, 1948, and gave money to help build the new Jewish homeland. They had little sympathy for the American Council for Judaism, a Jewish organization founded in 1942 that opposed the creation of an independent Jewish state. But despite these widespread feelings of identification with Israel, Zionism did not help people build a Jewish life in the American suburbs. Zionist organizations lost members beginning in the 1950s. Their schools, youth movements, and other activities could not compete with the suburban congregations. One of very few Zionist organizations that blossomed in the suburbs was Hadassah, a

SAVE THE LIVES OF THE ROSENBERGS......!

Julius and Ethel Rosenberg are doomed to the electric chair on January 15th. They have been sentenced to die in spite of the fact that the F.B.I. has admitted to perjury on the part of an important witness.

Millions throughout the world are demanding clemency for them. Important lawyers like Prof. Stephen Love of Northwestern University, Chairman of the Character and Fitness Board of the Illinois Supreme Court; D. N. Pritt, Queen's Counselor; Arthur Garfield Hays, have raised grave and reasonable doubts. Scientists like Dr. Joseph Mayer of the University of Chicago have questioned the scientific testimony and asked for clemency.

Trade unionists throughout the world have recognized the nature of the case, The London Trades Council in England, the C.G.T. in France, the G.G.I.L. in Italy, the trade unions in Japan, and many other countries, as well as unions in the United States like Ford Local 600, U.A.W.-C.I.O.; Building Trades Council of San Francisco, A.F.L.; International Longshoremen and Warehousemen's Union; Jewelry Workers, Local 1, A.F.L., and many others have called for clemency.

Join the Daily Forward, The Jewish Day, and The Jewish Morning Journal and such others as Dorothy Thompson, Max Lerner.

WRITE—WIRE PRESIDENT TRUMAN, WHITE HOUSE, WASHINGTON, D. C. ASK FOR EXECUTIVE CLEMENCY FOR THE ROSENBERGS.

ATTEND THE DISTRIBUTIVE WORKERS PRAYER AND CLEMENCY MEETING.

Chateau Gardens
105 East Houston Street, N. Y. C.
Tuesday, December 30th at 7 p.m.
Hear Rabbi Meyer Scharff
and other distinguished speakers

DISTRIBUTIVE WORKERS COMMITTEE FOR CLEMENCY FOR THE ROSENBERGS
1050 Sixth Avenue, N. Y. C.   BRyant 9-9694

This poster was printed for a New York City rally in December 1952, at which Rabbi Mayer Scharff spoke to help "Save the Lives of the Rosenbergs." Between 1950 and 1953, Ethel and Julius Rosenberg were accused of having given secret information to the Soviet Union, arrested for treason, and eventually executed.

women's organization founded in 1912 that raised money for Hadassah Hospital in Jerusalem and for other social-service projects in Israel. Thousands of suburban Jewish women joined Hadassah because they supported its mission—and because it gave them a comfortable social environment.

Will Herberg was a Jewish philosopher who had been a committed Marxist but turned to—or returned to—Judaism. In 1955, a year after the 300th anniversary of the arrival of the first Jews in North America, he published a book titled *Protestant, Catholic, Jew* that is one of the most important documents of American Jewish life in the aftermath of World War II.

Herberg explained why most of the secular institutions of Jewish life, like the socialist and Zionist organizations, seemed to have lost out to the synagogues. American society, Herberg wrote, accepted the idea that people differed from one another when it came to religion. Americans tolerated diversity in matters of religious faith but were much less comfortable with the idea of ethnic differences. Jews had remade themselves to fit the American ideal that said that people could differ in where and how they worshipped but should be pretty much the same in every other way. This observation applied to the new Jewish religious life of the suburbs.

Catholic, Protestant, Jew made another point that showed how dramatically Jews' lives had changed in the decade since World War II. Herberg claimed that Judaism had become one of America's "three great faiths." Public ceremonies, messages by politicians and government officials, and other depictions of American religious life now included Judaism right next to Protestantism and Catholicism. This was astounding. About 40 percent of Americans were Catholic. More than 50 percent were Protestant. Fewer than 5 percent were Jews. But now, when Americans described their country's religious heritage, they mentioned the two giant Christian groups and the tiny Jewish one.

What had happened to make it possible for the small Jewish community to be included among the "three great faiths"? Perhaps Americans were more ready to recognize the Jews in their midst because they were so horrified by what had happened to European Jews during the Holocaust. When it became public knowledge that Germany had murdered 6 million Jews because of their religion, many Americans responded by reaching out to the Jews.

At the same time, the United States was locked in the cold war with the Soviet Union. The two powers competed in many ways all over the world. Most Americans considered the Soviet Union and communism to be evils that threatened the United States. They also believed, like any people, that their own way of life was vastly superior to any other. And that way of life included religion, which the Soviet Union had discouraged and even outlawed. Americans boasted that they allowed all kinds of religions to flourish. When Americans of the 1950s and 1960s spoke of their tradition of religious freedom and tolerance, they emphasized the fact that the United States valued all religions and included everyone. As perhaps the most visible group of religious outsiders, Jews benefited from this emphasis on toleration. People began to consider Judaism an *American* religion, and society was more open to Jews than it had ever been before.

Anti-Semitism, which had been so powerful in the 1930s and during the war, declined. Opinion polls showed that the number of Americans who held negative attitudes about Jews got smaller every year. The

The National Conference of Christians and Jews appealed to Americans to forget their differences and to participate together in public programs that emphasized common ideas and beliefs. In the 1950s Jewish organizations believed that the best way to fight anti-Semitism was to combat all forms of prejudice.

surveys also showed that as Americans became more educated they held fewer prejudices against Jews.

The universities, colleges, and professional schools that in the 1920s had established quotas to limit the number of Jewish students now eased or ended the quota system, and schools that had never admitted Jews changed their practices. Jewish students flocked to them. During the 1960s, about 80 percent of all young Jewish women and men attended college, clearly taking advantage of the end of anti-Semitism on the campuses.

When these Jewish students arrived on campus they found something new: Many of the faculty members who taught their classes were Jewish. Before the 1950s it had been very difficult for Jews to get jobs teaching in universities. Yale University, for example, had not given a Jewish professor tenure in the undergraduate college until after World War II. Harvard University had formed a committee in 1939 to study anti-Semitism on campus. Its report concluded that "anti-Semitic feeling has operated within the universities. . . . it has made it difficult for Jews otherwise eligible to obtain initial appointment, and there is reason to believe, has retarded their advancement to higher rank when appointed."

The college teaching jobs open to Jews had tended to be in some of the new fields created in the 20th century—psychology, anthropology, economics, or sociology. Jews did not hold teaching positions in the classics, literature, or history departments, and Jewish students were discouraged from entering these fields. Even well-meaning professors pointed out that they would be unable to find work once they graduated. Long after Jews had entered in large numbers into law and medicine, university faculties remained closed to them.

That changed between 1945 and 1967. In one school after another, one department after another, Jews got teaching jobs. It was not always easy. Some departments debated whether it was possible to include a Jew. But gradually the barriers of this lingering anti-Semitism fell. By the end of the 1960s about 30,000 Jews held positions in American universities. In other words, about a tenth of all professors were Jewish. Some of them had been refugees from Nazi Germany who reestablished themselves in the United States. Most were children and grandchildren of the immigrants of the late 19th and early 20th centuries.

Jews in universities rarely taught or studied specifically Jewish subjects. Some schools offered courses in Hebrew or in Jewish history, literature, and philosophy, but very few students enrolled in them. Similarly, only a few Jewish students decided to enroll at Brandeis University, founded in 1948 as the first Jewish-sponsored institution of higher learning open to all. The founders of Brandeis University wanted to create a major research university where Jews would be comfortable and where they would not meet prejudice and discrimination. They succeeded—at precisely the moment when Jews were becoming more comfortable and experiencing less discrimination than ever.

Anti-Semitism was losing its grip as Gentile Americans came into ever-greater contact with Jews in neighborhoods, schools, and workplaces. It also weakened because Jews were now part of the mainstream of American culture. In 1958, for example, Leonard Bernstein became the conductor of the New York Philharmonic Orchestra and launched a series of televised "Young People's Concerts" that he hosted for 15 years. Many Americans also knew him as the composer of the very popular musical *West Side Story*, which premiered on Broadway in 1957. *West Side Story* took the plot of Shakespeare's *Romeo and Juliet* and set it in a multiethnic American neighborhood, making the point that ethnic hatred hurts all people.

Another thing that weakened anti-Semitism may have been the fact that by the 1960s Jews seemed to be more closely in step with the general

These students study on the lawn at Brandeis University in front of a statue of its namesake. Brandeis University was looked upon as an example of how Jews could build a great university, open to all, that still emphasized Jewish contributions to world history and civilization.

Arthur Goldberg, a highly respected labor lawyer, was named to the U.S. Supreme Court by President John F. Kennedy in 1962. Goldberg later resigned to represent the United States at the United Nations.

mood of the American people than ever before. In an era of general well-being and prosperity, more Americans embraced liberal politics. This made the Jews' political position and that of many Americans seem quite similar.

Jews overwhelmingly voted for John F. Kennedy in the Presidential election of 1960. Jews had voted for Democrats since the 1920s, but the 1960 election was special. For the first time Americans elected a Catholic President, ending a long tradition that had seemed to establish Protestantism as *the* religious faith of the United States.

During the Kennedy and Lyndon Johnson administrations, Jews held prominent positions in the government. Kennedy named labor lawyer Arthur Goldberg as his first secretary of labor. The child of Russian immigrants, Goldberg had grown up in Chicago and been the first person in his family to graduate from high school. He became a lawyer, defending labor unions against employers.

In 1962, Felix Frankfurter, who was Jewish, resigned from the U.S. Supreme Court because of poor health. Kennedy wanted to continue the practice of having a Jew on the highest court—ever since 1915, when Woodrow Wilson had named Louis Brandeis, someone had occupied the "Jewish seat." Kennedy kept this tradition alive by nominating Arthur Goldberg.

Americans had been deeply affected by World War II and by the terrible things they learned about the Holocaust. The example of Nazi Germany showed that prejudice might start on a small scale but could lead to unspeakable brutality. After the war, the American Jewish Committee and the Anti-Defamation League, as well as many local community organizations, set out to educate the American public about the horrors of intolerance. They sponsored films, books, and conferences that pointed out the irrationality of intolerance. They wanted to show that although Americans worshipped in different ways, looked different, and came from different places, they were alike in terms of character and commitment to the United States.

Both the national and the local Jewish organizations paid very close attention to any possible acts of anti-Semitism. As early as 1944, while the war still raged, the various organizations created the National Community Relations Advisory Council, whose job was to coordinate community relations work within the Jewish community and between the Jewish community and the general public. The council's name did not include the word "Jewish." The council wanted to advance good will towards Jews without drawing too much attention to the special problems of the Jewish people.

In 1947 some of the national Jewish organizations created a Motion Picture Project. It did not have "Jewish" in its name, either, yet its purpose was to encourage the film industry to use the power of the movies to promote tolerance of Jews and Judaism. The Motion Picture Project praised two popular 1947 movies, *Crossfire* and *Gentleman's Agreement.* Both squarely confronted the issue of anti-Semitism in the United States. In *Crossfire* anti-Semitism leads directly to a murder. *Gentleman's Agreement* deals with a more indirect problem. Gregory Peck plays a reporter who poses as a Jew and learns what it feels like to be the object of discrimination and prejudice.

American law reflected the changing climate and also made it possible for Jews to enter sectors of society that had long been out of bounds for them. In 1945 New York State passed a Fair Education Practices Act that banned discrimination in employment and education. By the middle of the 1950s, Michigan, Minnesota, Pennsylvania, New Jersey, Rhode Island, Massachusetts, California, and Ohio had passed similar laws. By the early 1960s, 20 states and 40 cities had enacted some kind of law banning employment discrimination.

Jews had helped make these laws possible by working through Jewish organizations with state legislatures and with private organizations such as unions, church groups, women's groups, and other ethnic organizations to win support for the laws. They also filed lawsuits when they believed that they had been discriminated against. In 1948 the Commission on Law and Social Action of the American Jewish Congress tackled the problem of quotas for Jewish students in medical schools. Because of its efforts New York State passed a law making such quotas illegal.

The new laws embodied the idea that when it comes to looking for work, applying to college, or searching for a house to buy or an apartment to rent, Americans should be judged as individuals, not by religion, national origin, or physical attributes. Their ethnic, religious, and racial identities were nobody's business.

This kind of thinking fit perfectly with the way American Jews in the 1950s and 1960s saw themselves. They were Americans on the outside. Their Jewishness they reserved for the private world of the family, the synagogue, and other voluntary associations in the Jewish community.

The idea of public equality and private identity also meshed with one of the great political and cultural transformations of American society—the civil rights movement. The roots of the movement went back to the 19th century, but the modern movement started in the 1950s when black Americans began to organize their communities to combat racism. They struggled to dismantle the official, legal system of segregation that was supposed to create "separate but equal" worlds for blacks and whites but in reality treated the two races as separate and unequal.

Blacks demanded that the society, from the federal government on down, recognize only one standard: an American one. They made an eloquent case that law and public policy should not categorize Americans and treat groups differently. Jews understood this argument. It made sense and fit their needs as people who also had been treated not as individuals but as members of a group. Jews also felt that helping to make the United States a better place was part of their religious tradition of *tzedakah,* a quest for justice.

Jews enthusiastically and loudly supported the African-American civil rights struggle. Some civil rights activists came from the Reform movement, which since the late 19th century had committed itself to the betterment of society as an essential part of Judaism. Others were secular Jews whose parents or grandparents had participated in the labor movement and the socialist causes of the immigrant generation. Still others belonged to the Conservative movement. Civil rights seemed to be a perfect way to link Jewish interests and values with the crucial needs of American society.

Jewish agencies and organizations were committed to the civil rights goal of making the United States more democratic. They believed that a society that did not discriminate against black people would be one where Jews also felt at home. Jews regarded participation in the civil rights movement as their duty as Jews and also as an opportunity to help create a more just society.

In 1950 the American Jewish Committee hired a black psychologist named Kenneth Clark to study and write a report on how segregated schooling harmed black children. Clark presented the paper at the White House Conference on Children. The National Association for the Advancement of Colored People (NAACP), the nation's oldest and most vigorous civil rights organization, learned about Clark's research, and the NAACP's lawyers asked him to help them in their

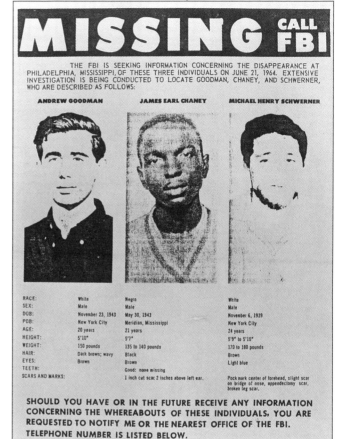

legal battle against segregated education. In May 1954 the U.S. Supreme Court handed down a landmark decision in *Brown* v. *Board of Education*, declaring the principle of "separate but equal" unconstitutional. The Court referred directly to Clark's research.

In the summer of 1961 handfuls of white and black college students challenged prevailing southern practices when they began "Freedom Rides" to desegregate buses and other forms of public transportation. The law said that black and white people had to sit in separate sections of buses. Of the white northerners who went into the South to publicly defy this law, two-thirds were Jews.

In the summer of 1964, called "Freedom Summer," still more college students went to the South to help blacks register to vote. A third to half

In the summer of 1964, three civil rights workers were reported missing and then discovered dead in Mississippi. James Chaney, a black man from Mississippi, was one of them. The other two, Andrew Goodman and Michael Schwerner, were Jewish volunteers who had gone to the state to help fight racism.

of the white students were Jews. Among them were Andrew Goodman and Michael Schwerner, who went to Mississippi. On June 20, they went with a black co-worker named James Chaney to the town of Longdale to investigate the bombing of a black church and the violent beatings of several of its members. They never came back from Longdale. Two months later the bodies of the three young men, who had been brutally murdered, were found in an earthen dam in the Mississippi Delta.

In 1965 a young black activist from the South named Marion Barry came to Washington, D.C., to launch the operations of the Student Nonviolent Coordinating Committee (SNCC), a militant civil rights organization. A Jewish woman named Liz Levy helped him get started by using her congregation, Temple Sinai, as the SNCC's base of operation in the affluent white neighborhoods of the upper northwestern part of the city. A wealthy real estate developer named Charles E. Smith held fundraising dinners for Barry and the SNCC at the Jewish Community Center (JCC). Smith helped fund many institutions of the Washington Jewish community and also donated a large sum of money to open a private school where students could receive both secular and Jewish education.

In 1965 Abraham Joshua Heschel, one of the greatest Jewish theologians of the 20th century and a professor at the Jewish Theological Seminary, linked arms with Martin Luther King, Jr., and other civil rights activists and joined the historic and dangerous civil rights march from Selma to Montgomery, Alabama. The author of a book called *The Prophets,* Heschel believed that involvement in the civil rights movement was more than just a way to make Judaism modern. He believed that it grew out of traditional Jewish values. Just as he would not violate the Sabbath or the dietary rules, so he would not stand idly by when other people struggled for justice.

Stories about Jewish participation in the civil rights movement tell of a time when American Jews seemed to be at the forefront of the most important and exciting changes in society. Jews today look back on the 1950s and 1960s as a kind of "golden age" when barriers from the past fell rapidly and Jews had access to neighborhoods, jobs, and educations that their parents could never have attained or even imagined. Jewish novelists

and playwrights like Arthur Miller, Norman Mailer, and Philip Roth achieved national and even international fame. Synagogue membership boomed, but religion did not keep Jews from participating in other formal and informal activities of their communities. They sent their children to religious schools but did not have to sacrifice much time or energy to give them some of the basics of being Jewish.

The nightmare of World War II—which American Jews rarely talked about in public—slipped further into the past. So did the poverty and troubles of their immigrant past. On the other side of the world, the nation of Israel had achieved its independence and seemed to be doing just fine. It made few demands upon the middle-class suburban Jews who felt at home in an affluent, increasingly democratic America.

Rabbi Abraham Joshua Heschel, a professor at the Jewish Theological Seminary in New York and considered by some to be the greatest Jewish theologian of the 20th century, marched with the Reverend Martin Luther King, Jr., in Selma, Alabama, in 1965 to secure voting rights for African Americans.

Chapter 6

At the Crossroads: Since 1967

Most changes in the way people live and think take place gradually. We do not usually see history changing before our eyes as we go about our daily activities. But sometimes particular years stand out. Dramatic events take place, and people realize that a new era has begun. Jews in America knew that 1967 was one of those years.

On June 5 war broke out in the Middle East, pitting Israel against Egypt, Jordan, Syria, Iraq, Kuwait, Saudi Arabia, Lebanon, and Algeria. Backed by the Soviet Union, Arab forces declared that they would totally destroy totally the Jewish state, or, as they called it, the "Zionist entity." From Egypt Radio Cairo announced, "The existence of Israel has continued too long. . . . The great hour has come. The battle has come in which we shall destroy Israel."

Everyone in Israel and in the Jewish communities around the world took these words seriously. The small nation had never been accepted by its neighbors in the region, and since 1948 these hostile neighbors had vowed to wipe it out.

France had been Israel's chief military backer and ally, but as war loomed the French decided not to get involved. President Charles de Gaulle declared that France would not sell weapons to Israel. Jews around the world talked about Israel being trapped. Defeat and destruction seemed inevitable

In June 1967 American Jews waited in tense anticipation as war broke out in the Middle East. They worried that Israel's Arab neighbors would be able to destroy the tiny Jewish state, but instead, in six days, Israel boldly triumphed, liberating Jerusalem and pushing far into Arab territory.

And then, in six days, the Israeli army achieved a stunning victory. Its troops dominated land and air battles, crushing the much more numerous Arab armies everywhere. Israel seized land from Egypt, Jordan, and Syria, and Israeli troops reunited the city of Jerusalem, which had been divided between Israel and Jordan since 1948.

In a war full of powerful symbols, none captured the imagination of Jews everywhere more than that of Israeli paratroopers gazing in awe at the holiest site in Judaism, the Western (or Wailing) Wall. According to tradition this ancient slab of stonework is all that remains of a great Temple built centuries earlier. Jordan had held the Western Wall until Israel recaptured it in 1967.

During the six days of the war, the Jewish people rode a roller-coaster from what seemed like certain tragedy to the euphoria of unimagined victory. American Jews, too, experienced a tumult of emotions. They mobilized for the support of Israel as never before, raising $307 million. They wrote, called, and telegraphed Congress and the President with demands that the United States help Israel. American Jews who had never visited Israel, belonged to a Zionist organization, or called themselves Zionists organized rallies to support Israel. Jewish college students who had never participated in anything Jewish flocked to mass meetings to express their sense of the oneness of the Jewish people at a moment of crisis.

The Six-Day War brought the fate of Israel and that of American Jews closer together. Militarily and politically, Israel became increasingly dependent on the United States. American Jews did not generally vote for candidates *just* because of their position on support for Israel, but they placed that issue high on their list of political concerns.

Equally important, American Jewish institutions became increasingly Israel-centered. Synagogues, youth groups, Jewish schools, summer camps, and Jewish community centers devoted much more time to Israel and its culture than ever before. For example, summer camps hired Israeli counselors to give American Jewish youngsters a connection to Israel. Synagogues and local Jewish fund-raising groups sponsored trips to Israel for couples, teens, families, and even Gentile local officials. They called these trips "missions," giving them a religious and spiritual aura.

Another event of 1967 received less press coverage than the Six-Day War but also heralded a change for Jewish Americans. On Labor Day weekend a small political conference took place in Chicago. The Conference for a New Politics brought together about 2,000 left-wing activists who in the 1960s had worked in the civil rights movement and the movement to end U.S. involvement in the war in Vietnam. They met at the Palmer House hotel to talk about creating a new political party to challenge both the Republicans and the Democrats.

Many of the activists at the conference were Jews. Jewish students and intellectuals had been deeply involved in the movements for civil rights and to end the war in Vietnam. They not only participated in progressive politics as activists but also provided much of the financial support that made activism possible.

The Black Caucus, one of many groups that formed during the conference, passed a series of resolutions. One of those resolutions condemned Israel. It declared that the Six-Day War had been an "imperialist Zionist war," and that Israel, a white European nation, exploited the dark-skinned Arabs whose land they had stolen.

These ideas and words stunned the Jews who attended the conference. They had come to forge a new political organization that cut across the lines of race, believing that their Jewishness and their political radicalism fit together perfectly. Suddenly, however, many of them realized that their vision was different from that of many of the conference's black participants. They found themselves in conflict between their Jewishness and their loyalty to the political movement. Earlier in the summer they had cheered Israel's triumph. Now they felt outnumbered and on the "wrong" side of the issue.

Until 1967 both Jewish and African-American activists believed they shared political goals. Both wanted to see the United States change from a society based on racism and exclusiveness to one that recognized the rights of all. Jews had participated in the civil rights struggle. Rabbis had been arrested and sometimes beaten by the police in southern communities when they went to help break down the system of segregation. But after 1967 one event after another turned Jews and blacks against each other. Each time the details of the incident became less important than the tremendous anger on both sides. Jews felt that they had been betrayed by those who had until recently been allies.

Several incidents illustrate the growing tension between Jews and blacks. In 1968, New York City schoolteachers—most of whom were Jewish, supported by their Jewish-led union—opposed the actions of the black independent school district in the Ocean Hills–Brownsville neighborhood of Brooklyn. The strike went far beyond a labor dispute or even a clash of views on education. It inflamed public opinion and became a struggle between two communities. A black radio commentator, Julius Lester, read a poem written by a black youngster:

> Hey, Jew boy, with the *yarmulke* on your head
> You pale-faced Jew boy—I wish you were dead

Riots erupted in many American cities in 1967 and 1968. African Americans—frustrated by the lack of progress toward equality and devastated by the April 1968 assassination of the Reverend Martin Luther King, Jr.—destroyed property and looted shops in their own neighborhoods. Older Jewish merchants owned many of those stores, and Jews had once lived in those neighborhoods. The angry mobs may have attacked these stores as "white-owned" businesses in black neighborhoods, but Jews believed that the anger was aimed at them as Jews.

In 1984, Jesse Jackson, a serious contender for the Democratic nomination for President, derogatorily referred to New York as "Hymietown" because of its large Jewish population. This upset many Jews, and gave rise to fear of increasing anti-Semitism among African Americans.

But actions became stronger than words in the summer of 1991 when a young black child was struck and killed by a car driven by a member of the Lubavitch Hasidic community on the streets of Brooklyn's Crown Heights neighborhood. Tension had been mounting between the two, very different, groups who shared this neighborhood, and a riot broke out as a result of the accident. Roving bands of African-American teenagers attacked their Hasidic neighbors on the streets and in their homes. A visiting Australian scholar, a guest of the Hasidic community in Crown Heights, was stabbed and his attackers were heard shouting anti-Jewish slogans.

Louis Farrakhan, a powerful figure in the African-American community, frightened Jews with his strong anti-Semitic rhetoric. Enormous crowds rallied around him, and his popularity was a cause of tremendous tension between Jews and blacks.

Jews and blacks also differed over matters of public policy. Jews were uncomfortable with government policies that took race into consideration. They believed that in the past it had been wrong for society to treat blacks and whites differently—and they felt that racial distinctions, even those intended to favor blacks, should not be written into law. Jewish organizations wanted to help those who had been disadvantaged and victimized by prejudice, but they opposed affirmative action, the use of numerical quotas in education and employment based on race. This placed them in direct conflict with many civil rights groups.

Since 1967 American Jews have debated how best to respond to what they saw as a new phenomenon: black anti-Semitism. Jews saw themselves as Jews, not just as whites. Most believed that they did not deserve to be attacked, verbally or physically, by anyone—but especially not by blacks, with whom they believed a close alliance had once existed. Jews too had been victims of racism, if not now, then in the recent past.

They discussed such questions as whether they should meet with Louis Farrakhan, the leader of the Nation of Islam, an organization of black Muslims in the United States. In the 1970s, 1980s, and 1990s he repeatedly called Jews "bloodsuckers" and described Judaism as a "gutter religion." Most Jews believed that such language had nothing to do with disagreements over matters of policy and politics. It was simple anti-Semitism, and self-respecting Jews could not sit down with someone who uttered such words.

When incidents flared up between Jews and blacks, some Jews wondered exactly how comfortable and how safe they really were in the

United States. The end of the Jewish-black alliance made them turn inward. They became disillusioned with their own past actions. Perhaps it had not been such a good idea to give so much of their attention to the problems of others. Many argued that Jewishness needed to be more spiritual and more personal than participating in causes for social justice, however worthy the cause.

They realized, too, that Jews still faced all sorts of problems that no one else cared about. Not all Jews had made the dramatic move to the suburbs. The elderly and poor had been bypassed by the prosperity that the rest of the community enjoyed. In most American cities, New York in particular, some Jews lived in poverty and felt that their fellow Jews had abandoned them.

A militant group called the Jewish Defense League (JDL) came into being in 1968. At first, its purpose was to provide physical protection for Jewish victims of crime in deteriorating neighborhoods. The JDL's leader, Meir Kahane, argued that the Jewish organizations and the police did not care about the Jewish poor.

The JDL started with 30 members. By 1972 membership had grown to 15,000. The group received considerable attention from the press because its members seemed different from most mainstream, liberal Jews. Kahane and the JDL proclaimed that liberalism had been bad for the Jews and that Jews had wasted time supporting the causes of African Americans. Jews, the JDL said, should take care of their own.

The JDL played a key role in speaking out for the Jews of the Soviet Union, caling attention to the plight of Jews who could not practice their religion. Soviet Jews who tried to observe Jewish ritual or to emigrate to Israel faced arrest. The authorities sent them to prisons and mental hospitals.

Some American Jews had known of the problems of the millions of Soviet Jews long before the late 1960s. But by the end of that decade, efforts to liberate them became a major cause of American Jews. Militant groups, sometimes led by the JDL, tried to take direct action, such as picketing artistic performances by Soviet musicians and dancers, or demonstrating at Soviet consular offices. Using the slogan "Never Again"

as a reminder of the Holocaust, the JDL vowed that Jews would never again be persecuted while the world stood by silently.

The JDL was not alone in calling for more aggressive action to help the Soviet Jews. An organization called Student Struggle for Soviet Jewry represented liberal Jewish students who felt strongly that Jews must help each other. It staged sit-ins in front of offices of the Soviet government in cities across the United States and disrupted performances of Soviet artistic groups.

Eventually the older Jewish organizations and the more established institutions joined the cause. Starting in 1970 Jews in Washington, D.C., mounted a daily noon vigil in front of the Soviet embassy. Marches, rallies, signs, and banners announced that American Jews cared about Soviet Jews.

Meanwhile, Jews in the United States faced no barriers to participation in society after the late 1960s. Jews were presidents of universities that had once banned Jewish students: In the 1980s Columbia and

Starting in the late 1960s, American Jews organized themselves to speak out on behalf of the 5 million Jews in the Soviet Union who could neither practice their religion nor emigrate to Israel. This Washington, D.C., rally held in 1970 was one of many gatherings called to draw attention to issues of global Jewery.

Princeton Universities appointed Jewish presidents. Harvard University and Williams College followed.

Jews could become chief executive officers of corporations such as DuPont, which had formerly excluded Jews. Finance was another sector of the American economy where obstacles to Jewish participation fell dramatically in the 1960s. Jews had been involved in finance since the 17th century but had always operated in Jewish firms such as Goldman, Sachs, founded in 1869, or Kuhn, Loeb & Co., a German Jewish firm that opened its first offices in the United States in 1867. But in the 1960s Jews broke out of the confines of the "Jewish" firms to take key positions in previously Gentile brokerage houses.

A great many American Jews had risen into the upper middle class. Lawyers, doctors, engineers, scientists, and academics, they had more education and earned higher incomes than almost any other group in the country. They had come remarkably far from the poor, excluded immigrants of the past century.

No Jew had sat on the U.S. Supreme Court since 1969, but during the 1990s President Bill Clinton's first two appointments to the Court, Ruth Bader Ginsburg and Stephen Breyer, were Jews. By this time, the press paid little attention to the candidates' Jewishness, which no longer seemed important or noteworthy.

However, starting in the 1980s a chorus of voices began to proclaim that the United States was—or should be—a Christian nation, guided by Christian values. Groups such as the Moral Majority and the Christian Coalition believed that their values, especially their "family values," had been undermined by popular culture, and they took this message into political campaigns.

Although many conservative evangelical Christians voiced strong support for the state of Israel, others distanced themselves from Jews and Judaism. In 1992 the governor of Mississippi, Kirk Fordice, declared that it was a "simple fact of life that the United States is a Christian nation." When asked if he meant to say "Judeo-Christian," Fordice snapped that "if I wanted to do that, I would have done it"; he later apologized. Conservative columnist Pat Buchanan, who was running for the Republican nomination for President, said at his party's 1992 convention that "there is a religious war going on in this country for the soul of America." He did not mention Jews in his speech, but his words and the thunderous applause they received made many Jews think of past discrimination.

Around that time some of these fears began to be realized when hate speech from far-right movements became more noticeable. Synagogues were vandalized and desecrated, and so were Jewish cemeteries. Vandals painted the swastika, the Nazi symbol, on public buildings. Many Nazi-type groups appeared, sometimes calling themselves skinheads; they often appealed to young white men. There was also a sharp rise in the number of militias, military-style organizations that considered the federal government their enemy. These groups expressed bitter anti-Semitism that struck fear into American Jews.

Since the late 1960s Jews in the United States had become especially conscious of the Holocaust. That had not always been the case. Immediately after World War II about 100,000 survivors of the Holocaust had arrived in the United States. They drew little attention to themselves and tried very hard to blend in, to forget what had happened to them, and to start new lives as normal, ordinary American Jews.

For a time American Jews did not seem to want to talk about what had happened in Nazi Germany. Every so often, however, something would disturb this silence. For example, in the early 1950s people around the world read the translation of a diary kept by a young German Jewish girl whose family had gone into hiding in Amsterdam during World War II. The family was caught and the girl died in Bergen-Belsen, a Nazi concentration camp. But Anne Frank's father survived. He went back to the attic where the family had hidden and found his daughter's diary. Once it was published, people everywhere hailed it as a moving account of the terrors of anti-Semitism run wild.

An event in 1961 brought the Holocaust to mind. Israeli agents in Argentina arrested Adolf Eichmann, who had been one of Hitler's high-ranking officers and had determined upon the concentration camps as the "final solution" to the "Jewish problem." Eichmann had arranged for millions of Jews to be sent to the camps, where they were systematically murdered in specially constructed chambers using poison gas. The Israeli

In 1961 Israeli agents kidnapped and tried Adolf Eichmann, a high-ranking Nazi official who had played a key role in the systematic murder of millions of European Jews. The Eichmann trial, which was held in Jerusalem, received much news coverage in the United States.

government put Eichmann on trial in Jerusalem. Americans, including Jews, sat riveted to their televisions watching the trial. Eichmann claimed that he had merely been obeying the orders of his superiors, but he was convicted and executed for crimes against the Jewish people.

Neither *The Diary of Anne Frank* nor the Eichmann trial made American Jews talk about the Holocaust. They did not define their Jewish identities in relation to it. In the late 1960s and 1970s, however, younger Jews began to take a greater interest in the Holocaust, perhaps because the current mood of political self-expression made them want to discuss issues that their parents preferred to avoid.

Events in Israel also inspired a greater awareness among American Jews of their place in world history. The Six-Day War of 1967, followed in 1973 by the months-long Yom Kippur War, created a serious economic and military crisis for Israel. Many countries ended diplomatic relations with the Jewish state. Arab countries stopped selling oil to the rest of the world to force still more nations to distance themselves from Israel. In 1975 Arab nations led the United Nations in passing a resolution that proclaimed "Zionism is Racism."

Jews felt increasingly uncomfortable in the world, outnumbered and trapped. Few in number, they believed that world events were conspiring against them. In this anxious time, the image of the Holocaust became very powerful. It gave American Jews a way to talk about their fears. They wanted to know more about what had been almost a forbidden subject. And they wanted others to know.

Suddenly a rash of books, articles, conferences, and movies about the Holocaust appeared. Jewish communities urged cities all over the United States to create Holocaust memorials. People interviewed Holocaust survivors, collecting accounts so that their experiences would never be forgotten. Some communities created Holocaust resource centers, and public schools in a number of states and counties created special units in their social studies courses to teach youngsters about the Holocaust. The field of Jewish studies blossomed on university campuses. Courses on the history and literature of the Holocaust were extremely popular. In 1978 the NBC television network broadcast a weeklong miniseries called "Holocaust." Tens of millions of Americans watched it.

In 1979 the U.S. government created a National Holocaust Commission, later renamed the United States Holocaust Memorial Council. This group's job was to decide how best to show the Holocaust to the American public. In April 1993 it opened the doors of the U.S. Holocaust Memorial Museum in Washington, D.C. Millions of Americans and foreign visitors poured in. More than 80 percent of them were Gentiles. The Holocaust Memorial Museum showed them where prejudice and intolerance can lead.

Jews felt a special claim on the museum and the memorials. They told what had happened to Jews who had thought themselves secure and perfectly at home in Germany. In a powerful message to American Jews in the late 20th century, the Holocaust memorials reminded them that even when celebrting their acceptance and achievement they had the lurking sense that the Gentiles around them still considered them alien.

What did it mean for American Jews to be Jewish in the last quarter

In 1993 the U.S. Holocaust Memorial Museum opened in Washington, D.C. Millions of visitors explore the history of the Holocaust and learn about this tragic aspect of modern Jewish history.

of the 20th century? How did that identity shape their lives? By almost every measure available to scholars who study rates of religious and ethnic participation, many American Jews had only marginal ties to "being Jewish." For example, most did not maintain membership in any religious or communal Jewish organization. They spent more of their time working and playing with Gentiles than with Jews. With a few exceptions, the classic Jewish neighborhoods had vanished.

After the 1960s Jews dispersed not only to the outer suburbs of the big cities where they had traditionally lived but to states and regions where few of them had lived before. There had never been many Jews in the South and Southwest, but in the last part of the 20th century Jews started moving to Florida, Arizona, California, New Mexico, Colorado, and even Alaska. Many of the Jews who moved to these places formed synagogues and other Jewish community institutions. Still, the fact that they had moved away from the established centers of Jewish life showed that they did not feel a need to live among Jews, as perhaps their parents or grandparents had.

Like many Americans, Jews of the late 20th century were less likely to join formal organizations than their parents and grandparents. Their contributions of money and time to clubs, institutions, and organizations decreased.

Jewishness seemed to have less and less to do with their everyday lives. At home they observed few of the traditional rituals. Only a minority observed the Sabbath, lit candles on holidays and the Sabbath, or followed the laws of *kashrut*. A few practices lingered, however. According to polls, many Jews attended synagogue on the fall holidays of Rosh Hashanah and Yom Kippur, and most continued to fast on Yom Kippur, the Day of Atonement. At home they still lit candles at Hanukkah, the eight-day midwinter holiday, and attended a *seder* at Passover, the eight-day spring holiday. The pollsters could not know, however, what the respondents meant by "attending a *seder*." Did they go to a lovely meal with friends and family? Or did they actually participate in the dramatic rite of retelling the story of the exodus from Egypt, in which everyone eats certain symbolic foods in a particular order and reads from a *haggadah?*

For thousands of years Jews have marked the Passover holiday with a *seder*, a home-based ritual with a text to follow called a *Haggadah*, special foods, and ceremonies that are repeated year after year. Here the host passes out glasses of wine. In the course of the evening, people will consume four symbolic cups of wine.

The single biggest concern of Jewish leaders may be intermarriage. In any culture the family is the basic unit that gives people a sense of identity and shapes their relationship to the outside world. If more and more Jews lived in non-Jewish families, then despite their ancestry those individuals might not really be Jews in any meaningful way.

Intermarriage was a fairly new concern. Until the 1960s most Jews married other Jews. Marriage with Gentiles was rare and usually meant shame and anger for the Jewish family. Jews who outmarried cut ties with family and friends. After the 1960s, however, outmarriage became more common. In the friendly comfort of suburbia, Jewish children got used to associating with Gentile children. Traditional barriers between Jews and non-Jews fell in neighborhoods, schools, workplaces, and places of leisure and recreation. It seemed natural for Jews and non-Jews to fall in love and marry. In a way, the increase in intermarriage showed how well Jews had adapted. American Jews were no longer a group of outsiders. They no longer seemed very different from their non-Jewish neighbors.

Experts have not been able to determine exactly how many intermarriages were taking place. Since the 1960s different surveys reached different

The newspaper *Der Yid* is published for and by Hasidim, an ultra-Orthodox Jewish group that came to the came to the United States in the 1940s. After World War II, small Hasidic colonies formed in Brooklyn, New York, particularly in the Williamsburgh neighborhood. They live apart not only from American society but from other American Jews as well.

conclusions. In the 1990s some surveys set the rate of Jewish outmarriage at 50 percent, while others claimed it went no higher than 35 percent. But everyone concluded that the rate was high. It had become commonplace for Jews to marry non-Jews.

The organized Jewish community debated how best to respond. At one end of the religious spectrum, the Orthodox condemned the trend. They took the traditional position that a Jew is someone who has a Jewish mother. If a Jewish man married a non-Jewish woman, their children could not be considered Jewish. Some of the more liberal Orthodox rabbis thought that the non-Jewish spouse should be encouraged to convert to Judaism. Then the children would be Jewish.

The Orthodox were less affected by intermarriage than other American Jews because it happened to them less often. They made up less than 10 percent of the Jews in the country but, unlike most other Jews, they still lived in densely Jewish neighborhoods and organized their lives around the observance of their religious law and ritual. Regardless of where they worked—and many Orthodox Jews held professional positions—Jewishness filled almost every aspect of their lives. Generally their children attended all-day Jewish schools and had few opportunities to meet and mix with Gentiles.

Intermarriage was even less of a problem for the 5 percent of the Orthodox called Hasidim, "the pious ones." The Hasidim were recognizable by the men's long beards, earlocks, fur-trimmed hats, and long black coats and the women's long sleeves, long dresses, and wigs. They lived in totally Hasidic neighborhoods, primarily in the Williamsburg, Crown Heights, and Borough Park sections of New York City's Brooklyn and in such towns as New Square and Monsey in Rockland County, just north of New York City. They worked and lived in their own communities. They did not watch television, go to the movies, or read English-language newspapers. They spoke English only when they absolutely had to and kept themselves apart not just from the Gentile world but also from less observant Jews.

At the other end of the religious spectrum, Reform congregations were most affected by intermarriage. Reform was the branch of Judaism least committed to the idea that Jews needed to maintain boundaries between themselves and non-Jews. In fact, Reform Judaism had appeared in the 19th century because of the problems associated with those traditional boundaries, such as observance of the Sabbath and dietary laws. Reform had done away with many restrictions, and most Reform children spent most of their time with Gentiles.

In the 1970s Reform rabbis started a campaign to convince the non-Jewish spouses in mixed marriages to become Jewish. They wanted to show that Judaism provided a rich cultural experience and that families functioned best when they shared a single tradition. Under Rabbi Alexander Schindler, president of the Central Conference of American Rabbis (CCAR), Reform Judaism committed itself to an Outreach Program to bring non-Jews into Judaism. This was something entirely new in Jewish history. For thousands of years Jews had discouraged converts. Having long lived with hostility, they did not want to antagonize the Gentiles around them even further by trying to convert them to Judaism.

In 1983 the Reform movement took an even bigger step, one that challenged Jewish unity. The CCAR declared that it would accept as a Jew anyone who had *one* Jewish parent, mother or father. By making this change, the Reform movement admitted that intermarriage was here to stay and that the Jewish community must learn to live with it. Some Reform congregations allowed a non-Jewish spouse to be a member or even an officer of the congregation.

In the closing years of the 20th century, "continuity" became a buzz-word in organized Jewish communities in the United States. Leaders and committed Jewish laypeople were depressed by the signs of dwindling Jewishness. In sermons, newspapers, magazines, conferences, and lectures, they asked whether anything Jewish would remain in a hundred years. What could they do to create a community today that would ensure continuity in the future? Rabbis, Jewish educators, and ordinary women and men who cared deeply about the future of Judaism in the United States looked with foreboding at the rise in intermarriage and the decline of traditional practices and loyalties.

At the same time, however, another story was unfolding. Just when it seemed that being Jewish meant less and less to many American Jews, a revival of Jewish life took place. Many of the signs of renewal had grown out of the social ferment of the 1960s.

One sign was the *havurah* movement. *Havurah* means "group of friends," an informal term that rejects a structure based on leaders and followers. The *havurah* movement emphasized the equality of all who joined. Groups called *havurot* formed in colleges and universities in the 1960s. They gave members a place to pray and to get together with friends in a relaxed manner without formal leaders and using new kinds of music. Many of the young people who joined had attended typical suburban synagogues in the 1950s and felt that those institutions paid too much attention to form and not enough to spirituality. Members of *havurot* in Boston, New York, Washington, D.C., Philadelphia, Los Angeles, and other cities asked for more.

Havurot did not have rabbis. All members participated in all parts of the worship service, which took place in rented spaces or in people's homes. They did not belong to any "denomination," and when questions of ritual arose they did not turn to some higher source but reached an answer by themselves. They felt free to experiment with new music, new texts, and new forms of worship. The *havurot* incorporated melodies from the Hasidic tradition, which emphasized highly emotional worship. They added meditation from Eastern religions and experimented with dance and movement.

In 1973 three members of Boston's Havurat Shalom published an immensely popular book called *The Jewish Catalog,* subtitled "a do-it-yourself kit." Second and third volumes followed in 1976 and 1980. The writers wanted to

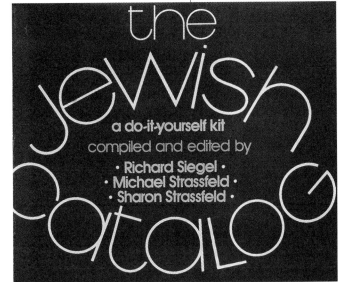

the Jewish Catalog

a do-it-yourself kit
compiled and edited by
• Richard Siegel •
• Michael Strassfeld •
• Sharon Strassfeld •

speak to the young Jews around the country who, like themselves, found little appeal in the formal institutions of Jewish life. They wanted to show that Judaism consisted of much more than the temples they knew in their suburban communities. "You can plug in wherever you want," they wrote. The authors of the catalog and the members of the *havurot* used the language and ideas of the counterculture to put young Jews in touch with the spiritual and cultural depths of Judaism.

The *havurah* movement never attracted large numbers, but that was not its goal. Its ideas, though, spread beyond its membership. Some large suburban congregations liked the idea of breaking down into smaller, autonomous groups—and they called these more personal units *havurot.* Jews outside the *havurah* movement bought *The Jewish Catalog.* Even fairly conventional congregations started giving the *Catalog* as *bat mitzvah* or *bar mitzvah* gifts to the children of their members. Religious school teachers taught from it.

With this emphasis on creative expression, the *havurah* movement helped the Jewish arts develop, particularly on the local level. Jewish music, graphic arts, theater, poetry, and literature grew out of the quest for spiritual meaning that the *havurot* inspired. These artistic forms were not Jewish just because Jews created them. They explored themes fom the

The Jewish Catalog was published in 1973. It called itself a "do-it-yourself kit" on how to live a Jewish life. Like much of the youth culture of the day, it was irreverent, and it helped readers to learn about Judaism and Jewish practices on their own, without rabbis or formal structures.

Bible, Jewish history, and traditional texts. For example, a number of American Jewish artists revived the long-forgotten craft of paper cutting, and *klezmer* music, an eastern European Jewish musical genre, became popular again.

Another result of the social ferment of the 1960s was that Jews challenged traditional gender roles. Traditionally all public rituals—leading services, being called to the Torah, reading from the Torah—had been performed by men. Only men could be rabbis or cantors. Women's roles had centered on home ritual. But women in Reform and Conservative congregations demanded a change. For decades they had provided much of the day-to-day volunteer leadership, and they had done much of the behind-the-scenes work that the synagogues and other Jewish communal institutions needed. Now they wanted a more equal and public role.

This insistence paralleled the women's rights movement in the larger society. Jewish women were deeply involved in that movement, and as they worked to end gender discrimination in the larger society they brought that same message to their Jewish institutions. They also left the home and the community organizations for paid employment, expressing interest in the same careers that their brothers were choosing: law, medicine, university teaching.

In 1970 Jewish feminists founded a group called Ezrat Nashim to challenge the male dominance of the Jewish community. They pointed out that men held all positions of influence in the community and said that Jewish women felt like second-class citizens in their synagogues. They showed how the language of Jewish prayer focused on men and excluded women. For example, in the traditional prayer book, still used in Conservative and Orthodox congregations, men specifically thanked God for not having made them women.

Change happened rapidly—so rapidly that an event in 1972 caught most Jews off guard. Sally Priesand graduated from Hebrew Union College, ordained as a Reform rabbi. She was the first, but by 1990, 167 women had become rabbis in that denomination.

The smaller Reconstructionist movement, which had been inspired by the teachings of Mordecai Kaplan, graduated its first woman rabbi,

The First American Woman Rabbi

The opportunity for girls and women to participate fully in Jewish religious life was an important change the 1970s. In Reform and Conservative Judaism, girls could receive the same education as boys and going to the same summer camps and youth movements. Jewish women began to demand that in Jewish life they be treated as the equals of men. In her own words, Sally Priesand recalls her momentous ordination.

In 1972 Sally Priesand became the first woman rabbi. She was a graduate of the Hebrew Union College in Cincinnati.

On June 3, 1972 I was ordained rabbi by Hebrew Union College–Jewish Institute of Religion in Cincinnati, Ohio. As I sat in the historic Plum Street Temple, waiting to accept the ancient rite of *s'micha* [ordination], I couldn't help but reflect on the implications of what was about to happen. For thousands of years women in Judaism had been second-class citizens. They were not permitted to own property. They could not serve as witnesses. They did not have the right to initiate divorce proceedings. They were not counted in the *minyan* [quorum]. Even in Reform Judaism, they were not permitted to participate fully in the life of the synagogue. With my ordination all that was going to change; one more barrier was about to be broken.

Sandy Sasso, in 1974, six years after the opening of the Reconstructionist Rabbinical College in Philadelphia. By 1990 the college had ordained 45 other women.

The ordination of women was more difficult for Conservative Judaism. Because this movement considered itself bound by *halakah,* Jewish law, supporters of women's ordination and gender equality had to struggle within a traditional framework. After many years of debate, with hearings held all over the country, the Jewish Theological Seminary (JTS) admitted its first female students in 1983. But the JTS and the Conservative movement had had to step outside Jewish law to do so, admitting that this change grew out of the need to be in step with the larger culture. Conservative Judaism did not want to alienate the thousands of Jewish women who wanted to be active Jews in a way that made sense to them.

Not everyone agreed with the decision of the JTS to admit women. A small group of traditionalists left Conservatism to found their own denomination, the Union of Traditional Conservative Judaism. Even today, not all Conservative congregations are willing to hire a female rabbi and give women full participation in rituals. But most do.

In Orthodox congregations, where even small changes in women's status faced severe obstacles, women have demanded the right to have separate all-women's services and study groups. Even as American Orthodoxy has grown stricter in recent years, most Orthodox institutions have realized that they must respond to women's needs.

In the past, Orthodox girls received inferior educations. For one thing, they did not study the Talmud, for the study of Jewish law and practice was thought to be appropriate only for men. But after the 1960s the gap between the education of Orthodox girls and boys narrowed, and as young women became more knowledgeable, their voices grew louder. For example, Orthodox Judaism never accepted the ritual of the *bat mitz-vah.* But since the 1980s Orthodox girls have marked their 12th birthdays with a special ritual. (In traditional Judaism, 12 was considered the age of maturity for girls, 13 for boys.)

Two other developments after 1967 show growing commitment and energy on the part of a minority of Jews. Enrollment has grown in all-day Jewish schools, formerly attended only by Orthodox children. Since the 1960s, however, the schools have begun to serve non-Orthodox Jewish students. They formerly emphasized Jewish studies over secular subjects, but now they give equal weight to both. Students come from all sorts of homes and participate fully in American popular culture, but they also receive intensive Jewish education. In the early 1990s about 100,000 American Jewish children attended these schools. Supporters of Jewish day schools hope that the day-school graduates will inspire others and become leaders in the Jewish communities of the future.

The other major development has been the growth of Jewish studies on college campuses. Before the 1960s individual professors had researched and taught Jewish subjects, but an organized movement to make such subjects part of the university curriculum began in 1969, when scholars founded the Association for Jewish Studies. By the 1990s more than 300 different schools offered elaborate programs in Jewish studies, courses that made it possible for students to learn about Judaism and the Jewish people. The goal of these courses was not to make Jewish students more Jewish but instead to offer serious intellectual study of the meaning of Jewish identity, past and present. The flowering of Jewish studies at universities may serve another purpose as well. Jewish tradition has always been based on knowledge; to be an involved Jew required exposure to ideas. Perhaps the intellectual stimulation that students experience in these courses will help them decide how to lead their lives—as Jews.

As America's Jews begin the 21st century, it may be that Jewish studies will help them make meaningful lives as Americans *and* as Jews. The act of learning may be the way to ensure continuity.

Glossary

Anshe "Men of." Men hailing from the same town or region in Europe named their congregations "anshe" and then the name of village or province as a way to remember the places they left.

Ashkenazim Germans, in Hebrew. It refers to the Jews of Europe, other than the Sephardim, or those who trace their ancestry to Spain. It is, however, not limited to Jews who lived in Germany or spoke German.

Ba'al Koreh Literally, "a master of reading"; the person who reads from the Torah scroll at public worship.

Bar Mitzvah Literally, "son of the commandment." Jewish boys at age 13 mark their coming of age by being called to the Torah, as adults, and reciting the prayers at the scroll in front of the congregation.

Bat Mitzvah Literally, "daughter of the commandment." Traditionally girls were considered adults, with adult responsibilities, at 12. They did not mark becoming 12 with any kind of public ceremony. In the United States from the 1920s onward, girls at 13 began to have some public event for this purpose.

Chazzan Cantor. The cantor traditionally chants the ritual service and is thought of as the voice of the community in worship.

Circumcision (in Hebrew, **brit**) A ceremony of initiation for Jewish boys, performed on the eighth day after their birth. A ritual circumciser, or **mohel**, surgically removes the foreskin around the penis. The origins of circumcision are traced to the book of Genesis in the Bible.

Gentiles Non-Jews.

Gemilass Chesed Literally "acts of loving kindness." This principle of Jewish life requires Jews and Jewish communities to provide assistance to Jews in need. It also refers specifically to the provision of interest-free loans.

Goldene Medinah In Yiddish, "a golden land." This phrase was sometimes used ironically and sometimes sincerely to refer to the United States.

Haggadah Literally, "the telling," it is the book used at the Passover **seder**. It contains the readings and songs around which the ritual is based.

Halakah Jewish law.

Hanukkah In Hebrew, dedication. This is a winter holiday when Jews commemorate their triumph over the Syrian-Greeks in 165 B.C.E.

Hasidim Literally, "the pious ones." A Sect of ultra-Orthodox Jews that came to America after World War II. They are notable for their uncompromising commitment to the rigid observance of Jewish law and their unwillingness to blend in with American society, even in their outward appearance.

Hevrot Informal groups of worship, based on the word **haver**, friend. Among the east European immigrants, most did not belong to established congregations with buildings, but they worshipped together in these small groups.

Kashrut The Jewish system of dietary laws, which regulate what Jews can eat and when they may eat it. Some foods (such as pork and shellfish) are forbidden at all times. Other items may be eaten, but the laws of **kashrut** requires that Jews not eat milk products and meat products together, and that they must wait for a designated period of time between eating one type of food and the other. These regulations also require Jews to maintain separate dishes, serving utensils, and cooking vessels for meat and dairy foods.

Kosher Acceptable. Food that is kosher meets the requirements of **Kashrut**. Other objects, like a Torah scroll, must be judged kosher as well, meaning that they were made properly.

Klay Kodesh Holy objects essential to Jewish ritual life, including a Torah scroll, its coverings and adornments, a hanukkah candelabrum (**menorah**), a **mezuzah** (a parchment encased in some kind of container placed on the doorpost of a Jewish home), a **tallith** (prayer shawl) and other objects.

Landsmanshaften Associations of Jews from particular towns or regions in central or eastern Europe. These were social clubs and also sources of mutual assistance.

Marranos A term of derision, meaning "pigs," referring to Jews who converted to Christianity in early modern Spain. The Spanish Christians often doubted the sincerity of their beliefs.

Matzo A flat cracker-like product made without leavening that Jews eat during **Passover**.

Mikvah (plural, **mikvaot**) A ritual bath. Jewish law requires women to immerse themselves in ritual baths, fed by flowing currents of water, before marriage and every month after their menstrual period.

Minyan A prayer quorum of ten, traditionally men, needed to recite certain prayers.

Mohel Ritual circumciser.

Parnass A wealthy individual, usually a merchant, who by virtue of his wealth governed the early Jewish communities in America.

Passover (Hebrew, **Pesach**) Spring holiday in which Jews mark the exodus from their slavery in Egypt, as described in the bible in the book of Exodus.

Pogrom A Russian word meaning a riot or an attack on Jews. After the

1880s these violent massacres became increasingly common in Russia.

Rabbi Teacher. Rabbis serve as the teachers and interpreters of Jewish law and by virtue of their knowledge of the law, they lead Jewish communities.

Rosh Hashanah The Jewish New Year, celebrated in the fall, on the first day of the Hebrew month of Tishre.

Seder Literally, "order," the **seder** is a home-based ritual conducted on the first and second nights of Passover, at which families and friends gather, and use the **haggadah** to retell the story of the exodus from Egypt.

Sepharad Spain (in Hebrew).

Sephardim Jews who lived in, or traced their ancestry, to Spain.

Shochet Slaughterer. In order for meat to be kosher the animal must be properly slaughtered according to specific laws. The shochet serves as a functionary of the Jewish community.

Shtiebel (plural, **shtiebellach**) Small houses of prayer, often store fronts, used by the **anshes** and **hevarot** of the immigrant generation.

Sukkoth Fall holiday, meaning "booths." Remembering their wandering in the desert after they left Egypt, Jews build huts and eat and sleep in them for eight days.

Tallith A prayer shawl, distinctive for the fringe at both ends, traditionally worn by men during prayer.

Talmud Containing the deliberation of rabbis compiled over hundreds of years, the Talmud represents the heart of rabbinic Judaism. Within it are numerous tales, legal decisions, and debates over how the laws of the **Torah** should be lived out.

Torah Literally, "teaching," the word Torah can either refer to the scroll read in synagogue every Saturday (and Monday and Thursday) morning that contains the first five books of the bible, or it can refer to Jewish knowledge in a more general manner.

Tzedakah From the Hebrew word for justice, **tzedakah** is sometimes used to mean philanthropy, or doing a good deed. In its original and preferred meaning, it implies an obligation upon Jews to act justly.

Trefa Medinah "Tref" means unclean or impure. Usually it refers to meat that is unfit for Jews to eat. Rabbis in eastern Europe feared that Jews would forget their religious obligations in America and so they sometimes called America a **trefa medinah,** or an unfit land.

Yarmulke (Yiddish) A skullcap head covering; in Hebrew it is referred to as a **kippah**. Traditionally Jewish men keep their heads covered all the time.

Yom Kippur Day of Atonement. Ten days after Rosh Hashanah, Yom Kippur is a day on which Jews fast and as a community seek forgiveness for their sins.

Chronology

1654

First Jews land in New Amsterdam.

1730

New York's first synagogue, Shearith Israel, is dedicated.

1740

Ashkenazim Jews from central Europe become the majority of American Jew.

1763

Jehuat Israel synagogue in Newport, Rhode Island, is dedicated.

1773

A group of Philadelphia Jews apply for a charter for the congregation Kahal Kodesh Mikve Israel.

1776

The Jewish population in America reaches 2,500.

1790

George Washington sends his letter to the Newport Congregation, promising "to bigotry no sanction."

1824

Dissatisfied Jews of South Carolina's K. K. Beth Elohim congregation briefly create an alternative, reformed synagogue.

1838

Rebecca Gratz of Philadelphia organizes the first Jewish Sunday school.

1840

Abraham Rice, the first ordained rabbi in the United States, arrives in Baltimore.

1843

A group of Jewish men create the B'nai B'rith, America's oldest national Jewish organization.

1851

First Western synagogue is established in Chicago.

1854

Isaac Mayer Wise founds *The American Israelite.*

1859

Board of Delegates of American Israelites is founded to coordinate the political activities of American Jews.

1861

Reform Jews found the Reform Sinai Temple under Dr. Bernard Felsenthal in Chicago.

1862

Union army begins appointing Jewish chaplains during the Civil War.

1870

Jewish migration from parts of eastern Europe begins.

1875

Isaac Mayer Wise establishes Hebrew Union College in Cincinnati.

1877

Formation of Adas Israel, a traditional religious group that was dissatisfied with reforms at their Washington, D.C. congregation. The group became known as Orthodox.

1880

About 150,000 young Jews move to America from Central Europe in a mass migration.

1881

Pogroms in Russia result in a massive immigration of over 2 million Jews to the United States.

1883

Emma Lazarus's poem "The New Colossus" wins the Statue of Liberty poetry contest.

1885

Reform rabbis issue a statement of the essential principles of their movement.

1886

The Jewish Theological Seminary of America (JTS) is founded.

Jewish Workingman's Association links itself to the Socialist Labor party.

1893

Jewsih philanthropists found the Educational Alliance.

Hannah Greenbaum Solomon establishes the National Council of Jewish Women.

1897

On April 22 the first issue of *Der Forverts* is published.

1900

The International Ladies' Garment Workers Union is formed.

1906

German-American Jews establish the American Jewish Committee, an organization committed to protecting the image of Jews in American society.

1910–1920

The Jewish Theological Seminary begins to move towards a new interpretation of tradition and the launching of Conservative Judaism.

1916

President Woodrow Wilson appoints Louis Brandeis to the U.S. Supreme Court.

1917

The Federation for the Support of Jewish Philanthropic Societies coordinates Jewish philanthropy and fundraising in New York. Other cities follow.

Zionists and Jews of eastern European origin found the American Jewish Congress.

1920s

Jews become a target of the revived Ku Klux Klan.

1922

Harvard University restricts Jewish enrollment to 10 percent of the student body.

1924

National Origins Act severely curtails immigration to the United States. Jewish immigration declines as a result of the low quota given to eastern Europe.

Louis B. Mayer creates the motion picture company Metro-Goldwyn-Mayer (MGM).

1927

Under threat of a lawsuit, Henry Ford retracts the publication of the anti-Semitic forgery, "The Protocols of the Elders of Zion."

1927

Approximately 3.6 percent of the American population is Jewish.

1928

Louis Wirth writes *The Ghetto.*

1942

American Zionists meet in May at New York's Biltmore Hotel and call for immediate Jewish statehood in Palestine.

1945

Reconstructionist group led by Mordecai Kaplan issues *The New Haggadah.*

1947

The Gentleman's Agreement wins an Academy Award.

1948

Brandeis University, America's first Jewish-sponsored university, opens its doors.

Israel declares its independence on May 14.

1954

American Jews help the National Association for the Advancement of Colored People win its landmark case, *Brown* v. *Board of Education.*

1960s

Jews move out of cities and into the suburbs in large numbers.

1967

American Jews raise millions of dollars in a few days during the Six Day War in Israel.

1968

Reconstructionism, the youngest branch of American Judaism, opens its rabbinical seminary in Philadelphia.

1970

Jewish Feminist group Ezrat Nashim is formed to express women's dissatisfaction with the male dominance of Jewsih culture.

1972

Sally Priesand becomes the first woman to be ordained a rabbi.

1973

The Jewish Catalog is published.

1983

The Central Conference of American Rabbis declares that it will accept as Jewish anyone who has a Jewish parent and has been raised as a Jew.

1984

Jesse Jackson, a contender for the Democratic Presidential nomination, refers to New York City as "Hymietown."

1990

A national demographic survey shows that nearly half of all new marriages of Jews are taking place with a non-Jewish partner.

1991

Riots break out in Brooklyn's Crown Heights neighborhood after a Hasidic man kills an African-American boy in an auto accident.

1993

The U.S. Holocaust Memorial Museum opens in Washington, D.C.

1998

American Conservative and Reform Jews challenge Orthodox control over conversions in Israel.

Further Reading

GENERAL

Ahlstrom, Sidney. *A Religious History of the American People.* New Haven, Conn.: Yale University Press, 1972.

Butler, Jon, and Harry S. Stout, eds. *Religion in American History: A Reader.* New York: Oxford University Press, 1997.

Gaustad, Edwin. *A Religious History of America.* Rev. ed. San Francisco: Harper & Row, 1990.

Marty, Martin. *Pilgrims in Their Own Land: 500 Years of Religion in America.* New York: Penguin, 1985.

RESEARCH AND REFERENCE GUIDES

Fischel, Jack, and Sanford Pinker. *Jewish-American History and Culture: An Encyclopedia.* New York: Garland, 1992.

Hyman, Paula, and Deborah Dash Moore. *Jewish Women in America: An Historical Encyclopedia.* New York: Routledge, 1997.

Marcus, Jacob Rader. *The American Jew, 1585–1990.* Brooklyn, N.Y.: Carlson Press, 1995.

———. *The American Jewish Woman: A Documentary History.* New York: Ktav, 1981.

———. *The Jew in the American World: A Source Book.* Detroit: Wayne State University Press, 1996.

Ribalow, Harold U. *Autobiographies of American Jews.* Philadelphia: Jewish Publication Society of America, 1968.

BIOGRAPHIES

Ashton, Dianne. *Rebecca Gratz: Women and Judaism in Antebellum America.* Detroit: Wayne State University Press, 1997.

Gurock, Jeffrey and Jacob Schacter. *A Modern Heretic and a Traditional Community: Mordecai M. Kaplan, Orthodoxy, and American Judaism.* New York: Columbia University Press, 1997.

Pasachoff, Naomi. *Links in the Chain: Shapers of the Jewish Tradition.* New York: Oxford University Press, 1997.

Raphael, Marc Lee. *Abba Hillel Silver: A Profile in American Judaism.* New York: Holmes and Meier, 1989.

Sussman, Lance. *Isaac Leeser and the Making of American Judaism.* Detroit: Wayne State University Press, 1995.

IMMIGRATION AND ASSIMILATION

Cohen, Naomi. *Encounter With Emancipation: The German Jews in the United States, 1830–1914.* Philadelphia: Jewish Publication Society of America, 1984.

Diner, Hasia R. *A Time for Gathering: The Second Migration, 1820–1880.* Baltimore: Johns Hopkins University Press, 1992.

Faber, Eli. *A Time for Planting: The First Migration, 1654–1820.* Baltimore: Johns Hopkins University Press, 1992.

Feingold, Henry L. *A Time for Searching: Entering the Mainstream, 1920–1945.* Baltimore: Johns Hopkins University Press, 1992.

Howe, Irving. *The World of Our Fathers: The Journey of Eastern European Jews to America and the Life They Found and Made.* New York: Simon & Schuster, 1976.

Mayo, Louise A. *The Ambivalent Image: Nineteenth-Century America's Perception of the Jew.* Rutherford, N.J.: Fairleigh Dickinson University Press, 1988.

Moore, Deborah Dash. *At Home in America: Second Generation New York Jews.* New York: Columbia University Press, 1981.

Sorin, Gerald. *A Time for Building: The Third Migration, 1880–1920.* Baltimore: Johns Hopkins University Press, 1992.

RELIGIOUS FREEDOM AND EQUALITY

Cohen, Naomi W. *Jews in Christian America: The Pursuit of Religious Equality.* New York: Oxford University Press, 1992.

Diner, Hasia R. *In the Almost Promised Land: American Jews and Blacks, 1915–1935.* Westport, Conn.: Greenwood, 1977. Reprint, Baltimore: Johns Hopkins University Press, 1995.

ANTI-SEMITISM

Dinnerstein, Leonard. *Anti-Semitism in America.* New York: Oxford University Press, 1994.

Feingold, Henry. *Bearing Witness: How America and Its Jews Responded to the Holocaust.* Syracuse: Syracuse University Press, 1995.

Shapiro, Edward S. *A Time for Healing: American Jewry Since World War II.* Baltimore: Johns Hopkins University Press, 1992.

JEWS IN AMERICA

Birmingham, Stephen. *Our Crowd: The Great Jewish Families of New York.* New York: Harper & Row, 1967.

———. *The Rest of Us: The Rise of America's Eastern European Jews.* Boston: Little Brown, 1984.

Evans, Eli N. *The Provincials: A Personal History of Jews in the South.* New York: Free Press, 1997.

Glazer, Nathan. *American Judaism.* 2nd ed., rev. Chicago: University of Chicago Press, 1989.

Karp, Abraham J. *Haven and Home: A History of the Jews in America.* New York: Schocken, 1985.

Levine, Peter. *Ellis Island to Ebbets Field: Sport and the American Jewish Experience.* New York: Oxford University Press, 1992.

Lifson, David S. *The Yiddish Theater in America.* New York: Thomas Yoseleff, 1965.

Lipset, Seymour Martin, and Earl Raab. *Jews and the New American Scene.* Cambridge: Harvard University Press, 1995.

Meyer, Michael A. *Response to Modernity: A History of the Reform Movement in Judaism.* New York: Oxford University Press, 1988.

Moore, Deborah Dash. *To the Golden Cities: Pursuing the American Dream in Miami and Los Angeles.* New York: Free Press, 1994.

Sachar, Howard M. *A History of the Jews in America.* New York: Vintage, 1993.

Silverstein, Alan. *Alternatives to Assimilation: The Response of Reform Judaism to American Culture, 1840–1930.* Hanover, N.H.: University Press of New England, 1994.

Sorin, Gerald. *Tradition Transformed: The Jewish Experience in America.* Baltimore: Johns Hopkins University Press, 1997.

Wertheimer, Jack. *A People Divided: Judaism in Contemporary America.* Hanover, N.H.: University Press of New England, 1997.

Index

Acknowledgments

Even a relatively short book requires the assistance of many colleagues and I would like to take this opportunity to thank them. First, I want to extend my appreciation to Professor Jon Butler for choosing me to write this book. He was an excellent editor and reader and I am proud to have been his choice among so many excellent historians of the Jewish people in America. Nancy Toff was a severe taskmaster, and as such a superb editor who kept me on track and challenged me repeatedly. Casper Grathwohl played an important role in seeing this book through to completion. My husband Steven Diner, a fine historian himself, read several drafts of this book and gave me many suggestions; I thank him, as always. Additionally, Joyce Antler, Robert Chazan, Aviva Kempner, Pamela Nadell, and Marsha Rozenblitt helped me fill in many of the missing pieces. Any errors are however mine alone.

Picture Credits

American Jewish Archives: 6, 12, 14, 17, 18, 24, 25, 26, 28, 33, 43, 52, 55, 58, 60, 64, 66, 70, 74, 77, 81, 85, 87, 96, 121, 123, 143; Courtesy, American Jewish Historical Society, Waltham, Mass.: 27; Architectural Archives, University of Pennsylvania: 108; Archive Photos: 129, 134; Arizona Historical Society/Tucson: 37; Balch Institute, Philadelphia Jewish Archives Center: 40, 45, 107; Courtesy, Beth Israel, Oregon: 36; Bluthenthal Family Collection: 57; Boston Public Library: 111; Bostonian Society: 59; Brandeis University, Office of Public Affairs: 117; Cincinnati Museum Center: 30, 39; Collection of the Supreme Court of the United States: 118; Corbis-Bettman: 73, 102; Detroit News, Private Collection: 78; FDR Library: 90; Florida State Library: 100; Hadassah: 50; Holocaust Memorial Museum, Washington, D.C.: 135; Institute of Texan Cultures: 88, 63, 38; Jewish Community Center of Greater Washington: 104; Jewish Historical Society, Small Jewish Museum: 124, 131; Jewish Museum/Art Resource: 13; Library Company of Philadelphia: 40, 45; Library of Congress: frontis, 10, 47, 72, 76, 114; Minnesota Historical Society: 112; Museum of Jewish Heritage: 82; Museum of the City of New York, Byron Collection: 56; New York Public Library: 141; Seattle Jewish Archive Project, Suzallo Library: 62; Society for the Advancement of Judaism: 93; Southern Oregon Historical Society: 34; State Historical Society of Iowa: 115; YIVO Institute: 63.

Text Credits

"George Washington Writes the Hebrew Congregation in New Port, Rhode Island, 1790," pp. 24–25: *Publications of the American Jewish Historical Society*, 3 (1895): 91–92.

"Constitution of the United Hebrew Beneficent Society of Philadelphia," p. 44: Jacob Rader Marcus, *The Jew in the American World: A Source Book* (Detroit: Wayne State University Press, 1996), 168–170.

"Letter to *Der Forverts*, 1908," p. 68: Issac Metzker, *The Bintel Brief: Sixty Years of Letters from the Lower East Side to the Jewish Daily Forward* (New York: Schocken, 1990), 83–84.

"Speaking of Greenberg: A Poem by Edgar A. Guest," p. 84: *The Detroit Free Press*, October 4, 1934.

"The Zionist Paragraphs in the Columbus Platform," p. 99: *Central Conference of American Rabbis Yearbook* 48 (1937): 98–99.

"The First American Woman Rabbi," p. 143: Sally Priesand, *Judaism and the New Woman* (New York: Behrman House, 1975), preface.

Hasia R. Diner	Hasia R. Diner is the Steinberg Professor of American Jewish History at New York University. She is the author of numerous books, including *In the Almost Promised Land: American Jews and Blacks, 1915–1935*; *A Time for Gathering: The Second Migration, 1820–1880*; and the forthcoming *Making Space Sacred: American Jews and the Memory of the Lower East Side.*
Jon Butler	Jon Butler is the William Robertson Coe Professor of American Studies and History and Professor of Religious Studies at Yale University. He received his B.A. and Ph.D. in history from the University of Minnesota. He is the coauthor, with Harry S. Stout, of *Religion in American History: A Reader*, and the author of several other books in American religious history including *Awash in a Sea of Faith: Christianizing the American People*, which won the Beveridge Award for the best book in American history in 1990 from the American Historical Association.
Harry S. Stout	Harry S. Stout is the Jonathan Edwards Professor of American Christianity at Yale University. He is the general editor of the Religion in America series for Oxford University Press and co-editor of *Readings in American Religious History, New Directions in American Religious History, A Jonathan Edwards Reader*, and *The Dictionary of Christianity in America*. His book *The Divine Dramatist: George Whitefield and the Rise of Modern Evangelicalism* was nominated for a Pulitzer Prize in 1991.